David
LIVINGSTONE

FROM AFRICA TO ETERNITY

SAM WELLMAN

BARBOUR
PUBLISHING

David
LIVINGSTONE

ISBN 1-59310-385-9

Cover illustration © Dick Bobnick
Cover design by Douglas Miller (mhpubarts.com)

Published by Barbour Publishing, Inc., P.O. Box 719, Uhrichsville, Ohio 44683, www.barbourbooks.com

Our mission is to publish and distribute inspirational products offering exceptional value and biblical encouragement to the masses.

 Member of the
Evangelical Christian
Publishers Association

Printed in the United States of America.
5 4 3 2 1

Livingstone's South Africa

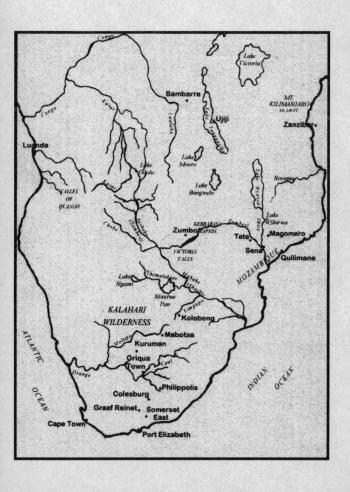

ONE

In a hillside above the village of Blantyre in Scotland, three boys sat in the brown winter-dead grass. It was the afternoon of March 19, 1826. It was the Lord's Day. There was a sharp bite to the cool air; the kind boys don't mind at all.

One boy had tousled brown hair and hazel eyes so lively they seemed restless even reading a book, which was exactly what he was doing. He held a tuft of grass in his free hand. "Yes, here it is," he murmured to himself as he glanced from the book to the tuft of grass and back again.

"Here is what, David? What is what, David?" asked a small boy squirming beside him.

"It shows a picture of this very grass and gives its scientific name, Charles."

"Father doesn't like you to read science," grumbled an older boy, who ripped up blades of grass and flipped them into the air listlessly.

"I don't see the harm, John," said the boy named David. "The book seems very truthful to me."

7

John just grunted. He was staring down at the complex of factory buildings on the river Clyde. Far down the river was the great city of Glasgow. John never saw it. David could think of no other word to describe the look in John's eyes but *dull.* John looked but saw little. He listened but heard little. Many of the boys and the men in the cotton factory where David and John worked had that same dull look.

David saw John glance down toward their home in Shuttle Row. John said, "Let's go home. It's almost time for cake."

David disliked being told what to do. Oh, he didn't mind obeying his parents. It was when other boys told him what to do that he got very angry. At the cotton mill, boys were always scoffing at the books he read during the lunch break: "Why are you so high and mighty? You'll never be anything but a cotton piecer like the rest of us!" That was about the only thing that really angered him. He used to scream at them: "I can think and act for myself!" But it didn't stop them from needling him. He no longer screamed at them. His anger had turned to pity for the poor lost souls.

"Are you coming or not?" grumbled John.

"Of course," answered David. "Come on, Charles."

They ambled down the hill toward the village of Blantyre. John walked ahead, intent on cake. David held Charles's hand. They walked under the ashes and immense oaks on the grand Bothwell Estate. They descended a bank to reach a three-story brick tenement building that was on another bank above the great cotton factory, which was really a monotonous group of long five-story buildings on the banks of the Clyde.

On any other day after the boys entered a turret on the tenement building they would have clomped up spiral stairs to the top floor. But today they entered a door to the first floor. By the time David and Charles looked down the hallway John was darting inside an open door. When they reached the open door, John had vanished within the people milling around inside the small room. There seemed barely room to stand.

"Happy birthday, laddie!" roared Grandpa Hunter as he shook David's hand. "Thirteen years old."

"Thank you, sir," said David, humbled by Grandpa Hunter's eighty years. He could never see Grandpa Hunter without thinking about the grandma he had never known, who had been dead for over thirty years. Why had God taken one half of their holy union so soon? Once a widower, Grandpa David Hunter gave up their cottage and field in Airdrie and came to Blantyre to become a tailor in the factory.

"I'll not be outdone by a Lowlander!" bellowed Grandpa Livingstone. "Happy birthday to you, David."

"Thank you," said David, slightly embarrassed by Grandpa Livingstone's pride in being a Highlander. Grandpa Hunter was probably just as proud of being a Lowlander. But David took after his father, Neil, who confessed to feeling like a Highlander in his heart yet dreamed of other lands beyond either Highland or Lowland. Of course his father, Neil, was in the room, too. His father didn't actually go to other lands like a missionary. He was only a wanderer compared to the men who worked in the factory because he traveled the shire to sell tea. David's mother was here, too. And Grandma Livingstone. After all, the celebration was being held in her apartment so the old folks wouldn't have to struggle up the stairs to the top floor. And, of course, now that David had reached his teens, he would soon join brother John in sleeping in this very room. There was a trundle bed under the grandparents' bed.

David's two sisters were also here. David liked being the big brother to Janet, an affectionate seven-year-old. But Agnes was only a bawling infant. There were nine gathered together this afternoon to honor David on his thirteenth birthday.

"I'll spin you a good yarn, laddie," said Grandpa Hunter. "It was way back in about 1750 or so when I was a thumb-sucker. My father, Gavin, who could write like Shakespeare when the other villagers could barely scribble an *x* in the sand and who was a bonny good fellow besides, wrote a petition for a widow to the high muckymucks in the shire to increase her allowance. Well, he might have appealed a mite too salty. He was arrested and convicted of insolence. In those days, a Scotsman his age who was convicted was put smartly on a ship bound for America to serve in His Majesty's army. Well, my father, Gavin, was a godly man and he had very wisely spent his time reading the Bible. He remembered well the story of David and Achish, the king of Gath, in Second Samuel. He thought to himself: 'Who could use a mad man?' And my father began to slaver like a mad dog, just as David had done. A sergeant who had seen a trick or two in his day was a mite suspicious. 'Are you really mad, my good man?' he asked. My father could not push the lie. He answered, 'Nay, sir. But I have a wife and three wee ones at home.' And the good sergeant told his commanding officer, 'This man is unsuited for America. We must let him go.' The officer, thinking my father was crazy, even gave him three shillings. And Father rushed home to my mother and we three wee ones. Three shillings was what Father normally earned in two weeks. But, of course, Father knew God wanted the widow to have that money. And the wee one named David Hunter ate his porridge cold!"

"Oh, Grandpa!" fussed Janet.

Both grandpas could tell wonderful stories. David's mother could tell a good story, too. And David's father, Neil, could, as well. Hours around the fireplace inspired storytelling. But they all deferred to the two old men on this day. It wasn't often that all the grandparents were there at the same time.

"Very interesting," said Grandpa Livingstone agreeably, "That was just about the time my own father fought with our own Bonny Prince Charlie at Culloden Moor. It was April 16, 1746, to be exact. My father fell that day to be with the Lord." His jaw tightened. "Perhaps we Highlanders could have beaten King George with a little help from the Lowlanders. . . ."

"Let's have some cake!" interrupted Grandma Livingstone. "We'll not start a civil war at David's birthday party."

But after the cake the two old men were telling their stories again. Grandpa Livingstone continued, "I can tell you the name of every Livingstone back for six generations, every one a true Highlander. A long time ago we were called the Mac an Leighs in the Gaelic tongue. We were in the clan of the MacQuaires on the island of Ulva. And it was one of our own grandfathers, boys and girls, who said on his deathbed to his family, 'I have diligently searched through the annals of our family. Never has there been a dishonest man or woman. So if one of you finds himself or herself doing a dishonest deed, you can not say it runs in your blood!' "

"Honest, yes," muttered Grandpa Hunter, "but not always agreeable. I never had a more unwilling apprentice tailor in the cotton factory than a Master Neil Livingstone you sent me." He stopped as the children glanced at their father, Neil, to see if he was laughing. He was grinning. Grandpa Hunter went ahead, "If he hadn't stopped to talk to my bonny daughter, the lass you children know as your mother, he would have completely sewed his thumbs together, the poor boy."

Neil Livingstone laughed. "And what a blessing she was. And still is."

David's mother lowered her eyes. "Neil is a blessing, too. He provides for us by selling tea all over the shire and beyond.

Our whole family is blessed by God. I just know it."

And the grandpas sat in two chairs by the fireplace and traded story after story until it was dark outside. They had pulled out the trundle bed for Janet, Charles, and the baby. Neil, mother, and Grandma Livingstone sat on the big bed. John and David sat on a braided cotton rug on the floor.

When the far reaches of the room got cold and the fire seemed to flicker banshees and ghosts around the walls of the room, Grandpa Livingstone said grimly, "That reminds of me of the tale of Kirsty's Rock. . ."

"Janet and Charles, it's time to go to bed!" commanded David's mother. And within seconds, with the baby in her arms, she was rushing Janet and Charles out the door to go up to their apartment on the third floor.

"I want to hear the story!" screamed Charles from the hallway.

"No, you don't," muttered David.

TWO

D avid shivered and braced himself.

"Kirsty's Rock. . . ," said Grandpa Livingstone slowly as he laced his fingers together in satisfaction.

David glanced at John. John was wide-eyed. They both knew the story well. David wasn't really scared, though—as long as he remained in the room. It was just like the room upstairs on the third floor where he had been born, the one room that was his family's home. In a few hours the six Livingstones would be sprawled all over the room on two beds and two trundle beds, wrapped in thick cotton blankets, sleeping as cozy as mice in a den. There was barely room to put a foot on the floor, even with John no longer sleeping there.

Grandpa Livingstone lowered his voice, "It was back on the Island of Ulva long before I gave up farming and left to come here. Ulva was a cruel rocky place. The word means the island of wolves. Great columns of black rock jut from the land like tombstones. The weather is not always misty and harsh. Just as the inhabitants are not always cruel and backward. But God has to struggle to keep them within His saving grace. Once a woman there accused a young lass of stealing a cheese. . ."

In spite of himself David felt a chill run up his back.

Grandpa waved his arms. "The lass denied it. 'I'm innocent,' she screamed. The woman in her anger tried to scare the girl with a butcher knife. The girl was indeed frightened. 'No!' she screamed and leaped to grab the knife. The two wrestled with the knife. The poor young lass was stabbed. Oh, woe is me. It was an artery that was sliced. There was no stopping the blood. The woman cried, 'By all that's holy it was an accident.' The villagers couldn't accept this excuse. The lass was lying there, white as any lamb drained of its life's blood. The villagers were so angry they tied the woman inside a sack and placed her on Kirsty's Rock. There the woman thrashed about, screamed for mercy, and tried to claw through the sack. But time was as merciless as the villagers. The tide rose and the sack slipped below the smothering waves. . . ."

" 'Stand in awe, and sin not,' " murmured Grandpa Hunter, quoting Psalm Four.

"Five o'clock comes early." David's father knocked the ashes out of his pipe into the fire. "Time to walk your Grandpa Hunter home, John and David."

That story bothered David more each time he heard it. Who sinned the most? The woman? The villagers? All of them? Why did Grandpa Livingstone always have to tell that story just before they all went to bed? He and John walked Grandpa Hunter home. David couldn't stop thinking about the story. Was it not true? Was it nothing but a scary bedtime story for children? He was afraid to ask. But he knew there were scary things out in the world. Was Grandpa warning that home was not free of risks either?

Home was almost sacred to David. He fell asleep that

night remembering warm verses from "The Cotter's Saturday Night." To David the poem was the best of Bobby Burns, because it so perfectly described his family, especially his father, Neil.

> With joy unfeigned, brothers and sisters meet,
>   And each for other's weelfare kindly spiers:
> The social hours, swift-wing'd, unnoticed fleet. . .
>   The mother, wi' her needle and her sheers,
> Gars auld claes look amaist as weel's the new;
>   The father mixes a' wi' admonition due.

The Livingstone children did indeed swap stories among themselves for a while. And, oh yes, David's mother made old clothes look almost as good as new. And father, Neil, certainly had advice to give.

> Their master's and their mistriss's command
>   The younkers a' are warned to obey;
> And mind their labors wi' an eydent hand,
>   And ne'er, tho' out of sight, to jauk or play:
> "And O! be sure to fear the Lord alway,
>   And mind your duty, duly, morn and night;
> Lest in temptation's path ye gang astray,
>   Implore His counsel and assisting might:
> They never sought in vain that sought the Lord aright."

David believed with all his heart that duties must be done—respectfully, too. He couldn't accept the joking and playing of other boys when they were supposed to be working. And, of course, he feared the Lord. In fact, this was a great worry to him. Because he felt he knew Christ in his head, but not in his heart. Where was the love? The joy? What choice did he have but to continue to seek God? But was he destined to be undeserving of joy?

> But now the supper crowns their simple board,
>> The healsome parritch, chief o' Scotia's food;
> The soupe their only hawkie does afford,
>> That 'yont the hallan snugly chows her cood;
> The dame brings forth, in complimental mood,
>> To grace the lad, her well-hained kebbuck. . . .

David didn't think living on a diet of milk, porridge, and cheese was peculiar at all. Meat? Bread? What luxuries. Would he ever know them?

> The cheerful supper done, wi' serious face,
>> They, round the ingle, form a circle wide;
> The sire turns o'er, wi' patriarchal grace,
>> The big ha'-Bible, ance his father's pride. . . .

That was indeed David's father, Neil, opening the Bible beside the fire, reading the Old Testament, then the New. The readings done, father Neil would bow his head and pray, just as the father in the poem. . . .

> Then kneeling down to Heaven's eternal King,
>> The saint, the father, and the husband prays:
> Hope "springs exulting on triumphant wing."
>> That thus they all shall meet in future days. . . .

David saw this scene every night in the home of his father and mother, even after he began sleeping at Grandpa

Livingstone's apartment. How wonderful home was. And home gave him relief from the factory. Hundreds of spinners and three times that many piecers made yarn where David worked. David was one of three piecers who worked for his spinner. The piecers had to spot broken threads coming off the reels of the machines called jennies and tie them before the flaws were incorporated into the yarn. A piecer clambered over and under machinery to mend threads—hour after hour. When the piecer was not mending, he had to watch for flaws like a hawk watched for mice. After many hours, the best of piecers was exhausted. But any flaw in yarn was held against the spinner. So it was not uncommon to see a spinner whip a groggy piecer with a leather strap to wake him up. And if the spinner got careless, he was whipped by a foreman.

In spite of stinging leather straps, factory work was boring. That was one reason why David sneaked books into the factory, whether the other piecers liked it or not.

One day a man screamed at him angrily, "Hey, you there!"

David slipped his books under the machinery. The vast interior of the factory now seemed very small. He looked up into a red face. "Y–Y–Yes, sir?"

"What do you have under there, you scamp?" yelled the man.

David couldn't lie to the man. "Books, sir."

"Let me see them," growled the man. "What? A Bible?" The man's anger evaporated. He began speaking so softly, his voice disappeared into the clatter of machinery. David had to read his lips. The man asked, "And what is this other book, laddie?"

"It's a Latin book I'm studying," mouthed David, so the man could read his lips. He hated yelling.

"Studying? Come with me," snapped the man.

David followed him into a room where the workers were forbidden to go. It was a room full of dials and gauges. Only the foreman was supposed to go there. So David knew this angry man must be the new foreman.

"All right," said the man in an almost normal tone of voice, "What's this about studying books out there with all that racket?"

"I was coming back from my lunch break, sir."

"Is that so? Did you get here on time this morning? I can check, you know."

"Yes, sir. Right at six o'clock."

"How long have you worked here, laddie?"

"Since I was ten, sir. Six years."

"Where did a sixteen-year-old like you get such a nice Bible?"

"I won it in a contest. I memorized Psalm 119." There was no point telling the man he won the Bible when he was nine. The man didn't believe him anyway.

The man raised an eyebrow. "Don't you mean Psalm 117?"

David laughed. Psalm 117 was the shortest chapter in the Bible. "No, sir. Psalm 119."

"The Psalm that's so very, very long?" asked the man skeptically.

"Yes, sir."

"Prove it. . ."

So David began to recite Psalm 119, all 176 verses, all 2337 words! Before he could finish the Psalm, the foreman held up his hands in surrender.

"That's enough," said the foreman. "I can't be off the floor that long. I believe you. What's your name?"

"David Livingstone."

"Well, David Livingstone," sighed the man. "You go right

ahead and bring your books. You might even leave your book open on a jenny so you can lap up a drop or two of knowledge on your way past the blasted machine. I'll not stop such a determined lad from learning his way out of such an infernal place as this."

"But Scotland has the most modern factories in the entire world."

"Entire world, is it?" The man blinked. "Well, you certainly see the bright sides of things, don't you? Yes, Scotland does have modern factories. But this here factory was built over forty years ago. Now when the whistle blows at eight o'clock tonight, you get yourself home to your mother, laddie."

"That's good advice, sir. But I must go to my Latin lesson at Mister McSkimming's."

"A Latin lesson with the schoolmaster?"

"Yes, sir. Until ten."

"You must have the energy of a dozen boys. No wonder you're so thin." The man smiled. "I can see real grit in your face, laddie. It's nigh the time you stepped up to something more responsible. I'll be thinking on it."

David went back to work. He didn't tell the man his Grandma Livingstone often had to take the book out of his hands at midnight with a mild "Don't you ever know when to quit?" and blow out the candle to force him to go to sleep. His brother John would already be long asleep.

Was it wrong to pursue knowledge so hard? Was he testing his grandparents too much? And his parents, too? His father sold tea all over the shire and beyond. He never came closer to the factory than the tenement they lived in. That's why it was perfectly safe for David to bring to the factory a book on the plants of the local shire, although his father had urged David not to read science. This advice troubled David, because when he took the book into the hills south of Blantyre and opened it to a map of the shire of Lanark, the book seemed perfectly true. There below him flowed the river Clyde that powered the great cotton factory of Monteith & Company where he worked. Married to the factory was his own village of Blantyre. Three miles upstream on the Clyde was the village of Hamilton. Eight miles downstream on the Clyde glistened the great city of Glasgow. And when David pulled a tuft of grass and studied it, he soon found a drawing of the same grass in the book. It seemed to him that this book must be written by a man of truth and righteousness. David had never yet found anything untrue in the book.

Yet he knew his Bible well enough to be cautious. "Forgive me, Lord. I am a sinner," he prayed. And he quoted First Corinthians, " 'Knowledge puffeth up, but charity edifieth. And if any man think that he knoweth any thing, he knoweth nothing yet as he ought to know. But if any man love God, the same is known of him.' " For a long time David had been afraid he knew God in his head but not in his heart. Did reading science make him unworthy of God's love?

How David loved to pursue knowledge! And yet, on the other hand, he had defied his father over knowledge only last week. His father insisted he read *Practical Christianity* by a man named William Wilberforce. David refused. And his father had given him the switch across the back of his legs. What had come over David to rebel like that? He didn't get home until ten o'clock anyway. He didn't even sleep in the same apartment with his father. It was just that he craved books on travel and science, and, of course, he had to read his Bible and Latin, too. He couldn't bring himself to even pretend to be reading the dry religious dogma of a man named Wilberforce.

"In the meantime," he said into the roar of the machinery, "I'll obey my foreman." He propped his Latin book open on the side the jenny. "It won't hurt to translate a word or two of Virgil as I run past."

"Oh, Socratees," teased a singsongy voice.

"What is that sound?" David asked himself. "It sounded like one of the sirens of Odysseus. Did I imagine it?"

Suddenly a bobbin struck his book and it toppled off the jenny. He spun around.

So that was it!

THREE

What do you want?" he yelled at one of the mill girls, who grinned widely at him.

In answer, she stuck out her tongue and disappeared behind some machinery. The girls teased him a lot in the lunch room, too. His mother said it was because he was such a prize. But he couldn't bring himself to believe it. If that was true, why weren't they more direct? If he were interested in a girl he would walk right up to her and tell her. But he wasn't interested. He didn't want to live in a tenement with a young wife and screaming babies. But what did he want? Would he ever see the world? How would he do it? He had no money. What was he going to do?

As if to reinforce his nagging doubt about getting anywhere in the world, it was three years before the foreman promoted David to spinner in the factory. Spinner was no great honor, unless one prized slapping exhausted piecers. He still propped his books up on the jennies and grabbed a sentence or two as he rushed past. Mill girls still knocked his books off with bobbins and teased him. And David began to look at the offenders not with exasperation, but interest. Was this his destiny? Would he marry a mill girl and finally one day stop reading books? What was the use anyway? And besides, he was still torn by guilt over loving to read science.

Then, suddenly, all his doubts dissolved and jelled like a perfect pudding. He read *The Philosophy of the Future State* by a Scotsman named Thomas Dick. Dick, a clergyman who was also an astronomer, convinced David in his book that God and science were completely compatible. After all, what was science but the study of God's laws of nature? And yet the pudding wasn't perfect after all. David still had lingering doubt because of his father's opposition to science.

One evening he confided to his father, "I can't find all the answers to my questions in this book by Doctor Thomas Dick."

"Philosophy?" His father frowned. He wasn't sure what the book was about. "Perhaps you could talk to the learned man. Isn't he a Scotsman?"

"Do you think I should go see him."

"Yes. Start early. It's a good walk to Glasgow." His father assumed all learned Scots lived in Glasgow.

The next morning David packed some food and announced as he left, "I'll be going now to ask a question or two of Doctor Thomas Dick."

"Do you have his address?" asked his father.

"Broughty Ferry near Dundee." David hurried off before the news sunk in. He was going to walk east across the Lowlands the entire breadth of Scotland to the town of Dundee on the east coast!

David had walked everywhere he wanted to go his entire life. And he fell into a steady pace of four miles an hour. At dusk of the first night, he crawled into the warmth of a haystack. Before noon the next day, he was knocking on the door of a house on a hill in Broughty Ferry.

"What is it, young man?" asked a man of about sixty who opened the door.

"I'm David Livingstone from Blantyre. I have some questions for Doctor Dick."

"I'm Thomas Dick. Come in."

As David walked by the man's welcoming gesture, he said bluntly, "This hill your house is built on doesn't seem natural in this setting, sir."

Thomas Dick laughed. "You are observant, young man. And direct. Qualities the Savior approves of. And you are correct, too. There is nothing natural about my hill. I hauled load after load of dirt with my wheelbarrow to build this mound."

"Load after load?"

"Eight thousand loads, young man." Doctor Dick saw his blank expression. "We are in the Lowlands. I needed the extra height for my telescope. I am an astronomer."

"You built your own hill?"

"Oh, everyone around here thinks I'm crazy as a tick." He shook his finger at David. "Don't wait for the approval of everyone around you, young man. Do what you have to do. And do it *now.*" He laughed. "But I needn't tell you that. I know of no other man, young or old, who ever walked across Scotland to talk to me."

David asked his questions about the Bible and science. Some people said the two were incompatible. Which was wrong then? Science? Or the Bible?

Doctor Dick smiled. "Such a common error. Some scientific observations are false because men are imperfect. But some science is true, too. On the other hand, every word in the Bible is true, but the truth takes several forms."

"How so?"

He inquired of David, "When our Savior asked 'And why beholdest thou the mote that is in thy brother's eye, but considerest not the beam that is in thine own eye?' did our Savior actually mean there was a plank in the eye of the man He was talking to?"

"Of course not. He was using hyperbole."

"And did Saint John in the book of Revelation intend to represent reality with symbols?"

"Yes, sir. I believe he did."

"When our Savior spoke of the five foolish virgins who let their lamps run out of oil before the bridegroom came to get them, did He intend that parable to be a warning to all the virgins of Israel to always keep plenty of oil on hand?"

"No, sir. It is a parable that means we must always be ready for the Kingdom of God even though we don't exactly know when it is coming."

"The Bible is the word of God, the wisest book we have or ever will have. But you must not be a fool with its wisdom."

David floated back to Blantyre. He felt as light as a dove. The resolution of science with God's word freed David of the awful contradiction with which he had struggled. How could two truths be opposed? In that false issue, he was certain now his father was wrong. Now, if only he could resolve his doubts about deserving salvation.

As if to match David's unorthodox behavior, his father left the Church of Scotland. This was not as abrupt as it seemed to those outside the family. Neil had agonized many years over the autocratic attitude of the ministers who were appointed by authorities completely unknown to the local congregation. Many of their edicts were based on traditions of the church and not found in the Bible at all, which David's father read constantly. He began walking the entire family three miles to Hamilton to an independent church. It was run by local elders. The minister was selected by the local elders. They preached that there were no elect, no predestined few who were to be saved. Salvation was by God's grace alone!

So at this same time, David found the greatest truth of all: Salvation was his. He embraced Christ. Christ was no longer just in his head. Suddenly, he felt deep love for Christ. At long last he felt the profound love for God that Saint Augustine wrote about so movingly. David felt a deep obligation for Christ's suffering. His inner spiritual life was born. The Holy Spirit had reached David Livingstone through God's grace. At last he was free. And his world seemed to explode with possibilities.

It was not long after his meeting with Doctor Dick that David too became a full member of the independent church in Hamilton. Membership was earned. For five months he had to be instructed by one of the elders. And soon after David became a member, he heard the minister read an appeal from Doctor Charles Gutzlaff for medical missionaries to go to China. To combine healing with the gospel was really living as Christ Himself. Yet, Gutzlaff's medical missions in China were revolutionary for the Scots of 1834. David's heart was completely won by the idea of going to China as a medical missionary. How much more could one man do than save souls for eternity *and* save lives here on earth? But for many weeks, David ruminated on how to accomplish this lofty goal before he told his parents.

"David, how can such an impossibility be conquered?" gasped his father, Neil, who then just threw up his hands. What was the point of expanding on how poor they were? Grandpa Hunter had died a year ago, not threepence to his name after his burial. And no one on either side of the family had prospects any better.

David said, "I've told no one but you two and the Reverend Moir. My plan is to save every extra penny I can for several years, then continue to work at the factory in the summers and go to Glasgow during the winter session to study medicine. It costs twelve pounds a session at Anderson College."

"Twelve pounds!" His father looked faint. "And you make five shillings a week? That's one pound a month. That's exactly one year's wages. And that's if you could save every penny. Impossible!"

His mother smiled. "I always knew David was special. There are so few factory boys who can even read. . . ."

"Not one in ten," muttered Neil, still numb.

Mother added, "There are so few factory boys who study Latin. . . ."

Neil grunted. "What factory boy can work fourteen hours a day, sweating like a dray horse, then run into the cold Scottish night to study Latin? Only one in a thousand and we're looking at him."

Mother smiled. "Yes. A boy who studied books until they were taken out of his hands at midnight. . ."

"And still got to work every morning on time," added Neil proudly. "He's no boy now, but a man."

Mother said, "John will have to help David."

"But how can John help?" asked David. "He has a family."

"It's tradition," snapped Neil. "The oldest son must. . ."

"Do you mean you approve, Father?" interrupted David.

Neil laughed. "I guess I do. You've got all us skeptics scheming and planning the impossible already. There's not another man in Scotland like you, David."

David was twenty-three in the fall of 1836 when his father Neil walked the snowy road into Glasgow with him, helping carry clothes and books. David rented a room for two shillings a week, found it unsatisfactory, and soon moved to another boarding house for two shillings and sixpence. So he added living expenses during each session of six pounds. But he had planned long and well and remembered the Lord's sermon on the mount in Matthew: "Do not worry about your life, what you will eat or drink; or about your body, what you will wear."

Being a student was ecstasy. "What joy!" he cried to God. "For thirteen years I worked fourteen hours a day so I could study for a few hours a day. Now I can study every waking hour of the day. This is truly paradise on earth. Praise the Lord for this joy."

He milked every minute out of every day. He walked to Glasgow University for Greek classes and to Congregational College for lectures on religion. But medicine and chemistry at Anderson College occupied most of his time. He had to learn anatomy and surgery by dissecting corpses. He learned to diagnose chest diseases with a new instrument that every physician was talking about: the stethoscope. Now the doctor could hear air rushing through the lungs or hear gurgling blood pulsing from the heart.

After his first session, he returned to Blantyre to work in the factory once again as a spinner. Also that summer, he applied to the London Missionary Society. It had missions in the South Seas, West Indies, India, Africa, and, best of all, China. And the Society had no religious dogma. It pushed no religion but the gospel.

Early in his second session at Glasgow, the Society sent him a list of questions to answer. Two answers David worked especially hard to articulate. On what he thought were the duties of a missionary, he answered:

His duties chiefly are, I apprehend, to endeavor by every means in his power to make known the gospel by preaching, exhortation, conversation, instruction of the young; improving, so far as in his power, the temporal condition of those among whom he labors, by introducing the arts and sciences of civilization, and doing everything in his power to commend Christianity to their hearts and consciences.

Another answer, to a question about his attitude toward marriage, was no less definite:

Unmarried; under no engagement relating to marriage, never made proposals of marriage, nor conducted myself to any woman as to cause her to suspect that I intended anything related to marriage; and, so far as my present wishes are concerned, I should prefer going out unmarried, that I might be without that care which the concerns of a family necessarily induce and give myself wholly to the work.

Young ladies were not attracted to him, either. He knew that well enough. He was tall for his time at five feet eight inches. He had a manly build: large in the chest and shoulders, otherwise trim. He had thick brown hair and intelligent soulful eyes. In one of her more tactless moments, his sister Janet had told him why young ladies were not drawn to him. It was his earnestness, his resolve, his fortitude, his tenacity that drew in and dimpled his chin and made him seem humorless. David Livingstone was not a bonny lad. His beauty was all inside, Janet added.

In the meantime, David was conscious of no loss at all.

He continued his studies, no small benefit of which were the friendships he developed with students and faculty. The assistant to the chemistry professor was a young man named James Young. David and he became good friends, Young even showing him how to operate a lathe and do simple carpentry. Two young sons of the mathematics professor, James and William Thomson, frequented the chemistry lab, too.

One day David overheard Young telling the boys, "He has more true trust in God, more of the true spirit of Christ, more true honesty, more purity of character, more unselfish love for others than any other man I've ever known."

"That sounds a bit thick," objected one of the boys.

"I've seen a good many men. I'm not saying it lightly," answered Young.

David shook his head. "Are you speaking of Professor Thomson, the boys' father?"

He was puzzled by their embarrassed silence. Later he began to suspect Young had been talking about him. What praise! Was it possible? Was he held in such high regard? All his life he had been scorned and ridiculed and teased by his peers in the factory. Was it only the complacent and fearful who scorned him? Was it only his fellow risk-takers who appreciated him? But he decided then and there he must not hate those who scorned him. After all, the Lord's own family and friends thought He was insane when they first heard about His ministry in Galilee. A passage in the third chapter of Mark said: "When his friends heard of it, they went out to lay hold on him: for they said, "He is beside himself." David soon learned his performance at Glasgow impressed his townsmen, too. He was a young man who made Blantyre and Hamilton proud, they said. Men like the lace manufacturer Henry Drummond and the draper Fergus Ferguson realized the

Mission Society's gain was going to be their loss. But to David it came as a complete surprise near the completion of his two years of studies to be offered a teaching job in the shire of Lanark for 150 pounds a year. It was a tremendous sum of money to him, more than ten times what he had ever earned before. But teaching was not being a medical missionary. He turned the offer down.

By the fall of 1838, David was north of London, lodging with other students in the small market town of Chipping Ongar. He had been accepted by the London Missionary Society. It seemed a dream to be walking the environs of London. With another student, Joseph Moore, he visited the buried heroes at Westminster Abbey, watched the changing of the guard at Buckingham Palace, and admired the Gothic spires of the Houses of Parliament. Was it really true that he, the poor Scots boy from the aging factories of Blantyre, would become an extension of this grandeur?

"Yes, by God's grace," he murmured.

But it would take determination. After all, he was no missionary yet. He was only beginning three months of probation. Rev. Richard Cecil was to make sure David was proficient in Latin, Greek, and theology before he began more formal training. Some students would continue in theology at nearby Cheshunt College. Some students like David were to go to London for more medical training. But there was the constant threat of failure. Only the very best students were allowed to go on with formal training. Of course, someone who failed could still be sent to the missions after acquiring skills in carpentry and bricklaying to work for the real missionaries. Or one could simply drop out of sight.

His fellow student Joseph Moore asked David, "What if we don't make it? Will you go to China as a bricklayer?"

"Of course," answered David. "But if God wants me to practice some medicine after I get there, I'll do it."

"The practical Scotsman," said Moore approvingly, but David could see he was surprised nonetheless. David seemed too docile to think such rebellious things.

Once David walked to London on an errand for his brother John, who was now selling lace. David was to see who would be interested in buying John's wares. It was twenty-seven miles to London, so he started before sunrise. The country of Enfield and Harringay was low farmland. In the darkness, he fell into a ditch on the way, dirtying his clothes. He continued through Islington and Camden right into the heart of London. Then he walked the streets, visiting merchant after merchant. On his trek back, he came upon a woman who had been thrown from a gig. He helped carry her into a house where he examined her for broken bones. At that point, any other man would have found shelter for the night. But David was expected back at Chipping Ongar. It was a new day by the time he arrived, having walked nonstop nearly seventy miles.

"You seem under the weather, Livingstone," noted Rev. Cecil the next morning. "What did you do in London? Never mind. You needn't answer that."

David didn't make any excuses for himself. But he was worried. Rev. Cecil didn't seem to recognize his better qualities, as others had. The reverend worked hard with him to get his Latin and Greek up to snuff, frowning all the while. He only grudgingly admitted David's theology was simple but sound. He even questioned David's motivation, even though every time David was called upon to lead a prayer, he concluded, "Let us imitate Christ in all His inimitable perfections."

There was another qualification to be a missionary. It was too critical to ignore. Every missionary had to preach the gospel. Each student had to write his sermon, then subject it to Rev. Cecil's persnickety review. After the reverend's inevitable revisions the student memorized the approved sermon and delivered it passionately to a local congregation. David's opportunity came when the minister at a church in Stanford Rivers became ill. David was told to deliver the evening sermon. He read through his approved sermon one last time and mounted the podium.

"Good evening, friends. . . ," he began.

His mind immediately went as black as midnight.

FOUR

David's mind buzzed with horror: He mustn't fail his sermon!

His logic was impeccable. Even his memory was impenetrable. How could this happen to someone who memorized the 119th Psalm? If only he could remember the first sentence. That would be the spark to set him ablaze. He had to remember it. His faltering way of speaking was one of Rev. Cecil's main criticisms of him. What was the first sentence? Suddenly he noticed Rev. Cecil in the front pew. His eyes were lowered in disappointment, but it seemed a disappointment he had expected. Behind him was Rev. Isaac Taylor, who had befriended David. Isaac seemed breathless, his face deathly pale, as he waited for David to continue.

David stammered, "Friends, I have forgotten all I had to say." He rushed out of the chapel, smothered by the silence of the congregation.

What humiliation. He had failed. And he had failed Rev. Cecil. And he had even let down Rev. Taylor, whom he had walked with in the countryside, discussing botany and everything else that crossed their path. How could David have suffered such a setback?

"Has God abandoned me?" he cried.

He went back to his room and opened his Bible. He remembered well a saint in the Bible who seemed to have a similar problem, but David always felt insignificant, even a little sacrilegious, when he was bold enough to apply what happened to saints to himself. But there it was in the fourth chapter of Exodus:

> And Moses said unto the LORD, O my LORD, I am
> not eloquent, neither heretofore, nor since thou has
> spoken unto thy servant: but I am slow of speech,
> and of a slow tongue. And the LORD said unto
> him, Who hath made man's mouth? or who mak-
> eth the dumb, or deaf, or the seeing, or the blind?
> have not I the LORD? Now therefore go, and I
> will be with thy mouth, and teach thee what thou
> shalt say.

David closed his Bible. "I must trust God," he told himself. "For some reason He did not want me to speak today. I must be too proud."

It was no surprise when Rev. Cecil solemnly came to him later. "Three months of probation is over, Livingstone. I am required to make my recommendation. In view of your inability to deliver a sermon and your generally halting manner of speaking, I will not be able to recommend you."

David thought the unthinkable. He felt like God had kicked him in the teeth. He left his room in a daze. He wandered the grounds. He made excuses for himself. It was his cursed uvula, the fleshy lobe hanging down from the back of his palate. It was too large. He hadn't realized it until he started studying medicine. It made his speech thick and indistinct. It worried him. The worry threw him off his stride. That was it. It was not God. It was a medical problem. . . .

A voice trailed him, "Livingstone?"

"Huh?" He turned to see Joseph Moore. "I've failed, Moore."

"Me, too."

"You, too!" Why was it he felt better when a friend joined his misery? God forgive him. "What are we going to do, Moore?"

"Keep trying."

"What do you mean?"

"Rev. Cecil said I was getting a second chance. Didn't he tell you that?"

"No." David's last hopes crumbled into dust.

"He must have forgot. Surely you'll get a second chance. You're so highly regarded here."

"What an inflated assessment." David laughed bitterly. "Your friendship has blinded you."

"I heard Rev. Isaac Taylor and his son talking about you the other day. One of them said 'When Livingstone walks he has a very particular stride, solid and determined, not fast, not slow—his stride simply guarantees *he is going to get there!*'"

David raised an eyebrow. "I guess that could be considered a compliment—if I were to become a postman delivering mail. But thanks anyway, Moore."

"I heard another fellow say you have charm, which despite your ungainly ways, attracts almost everyone."

"Thanks again. . .I think." David stifled a chuckle at the flawed compliments.

"I heard another fellow say you are kind and gentle, both in word and deed. Always ready with a comforting word. Or an act of sympathy."

"Stop, Moore. Your words are appreciated. But it doesn't change the fact that I must leave. . . ."

He walked in the countryside that afternoon, feeling very foolish. He had dreamed how he could convince the Missionary Society that he should go to China and not some other country. What a presumptuous fool he had been. He was not even going to become a missionary. The enormity of his failure grew on him. What about all his friends back in Scotland who had helped him? And now to top it off, he was wallowing in self-pity. What was happening to him?

The Reverend Cecil was waiting in his room when he returned. "I must speak with you, Livingstone."

"Of course," replied David curtly. Was he now going to be lectured on his multitude of shortcomings? Was he going to be told which paths were left for him to follow now? Was it to be bricklaying or carpentry? "Oh, Jesus," he prayed, "relieve me of this bitterness."

"They tell me you worked in a cotton factory fourteen hours a day, six days a week, for thirteen years."

"I was very lucky to have that honest job," answered David defensively. Then he wished he had asked who *they* were. Had someone spoken in his behalf? And what was the Rev. getting at? Was he going to ask David to apply his spinning skills in some backward country?

"I've judged you as if you came to me from a school for the well-to-do, like Eton. I must admit I have been severe with you. For that I am sorry. See me tomorrow morning, and we will discuss your next sermon."

"Next sermon?" David was stunned. A second chance!

Praise the Lord. And praise whoever might have spoken in his behalf. "Could you tell me who spoke in my behalf, sir?"

"It would take too long."

David worked very hard over the next several months, hard enough to realize he was finally going to pass muster with Rev. Cecil—despite his halting, barely adequate sermons. He even met a young lady named Catherine. She was wonderful to him. He had never met anyone so lively and captivating. She bubbled with life. She made him giddy with desire. He would be her slave. All his ideas about being celibate evaporated. He must marry her. But as fickle as a playful cat, she suddenly released him. And it seemed like overnight, she was engaged to another student. Once again he felt like a fool.

In May of 1839, he wrote his sister Janet:

> Let us seek—and with the conviction that we cannot do without it—that all selfishness be extirpated, pride banished, unbelief driven from the mind, every idol dethroned, and everything hostile to holiness and opposed to the divine will crucified; that "holiness to the Lord" may be engraven on the heart, and evermore characterize our whole conduct.

He concluded his letter with an impassioned argument that God grants blessings only to those with a willing mind. If that is lacking, all is lost. If the will to serve God is there, who knows the limits of what a person can do through God, the Creator who can do anything.

David's faith kept him afloat. He recovered from the rejection of Catherine. That was fortunate because he was more fit to handle his next disappointment: England was having trouble with China over opium. The situation in China was explosive. The London Missionary Society was not going to send any more missionaries to China until the problem was resolved!

"What are you going to do now, Livingstone? You had your heart set on China," commiserated Joseph Moore.

"God will surely provide the answer," said David, but he was shaken. He was often shaken, but to show it meant showing others a lack of trust in God.

A missionary named Robert Moffat was in London after years in South Africa. Moffat said that from his mission he could see in the distant north the smoke from a thousand villages! David was shocked. That was the exact opposite of what he had been told: The interior of Africa was a wasteland. David began following Moffat on his lecture tour around the London area. Soon Moffat knew him well. David would approach him after each talk, always with more questions. David knew virtually nothing about Africa. How could any European know anything? After 300 years Europeans had only poked around the shorelines. The southern half of Africa, in particular, had few good harbors. Its rivers were not navigable by any vessel larger than a canoe. The interior was a mystery.

David soon heard Rev. Cecil's thoughts on where he should go. "China is closed to you indefinitely, Livingstone. We presently have missions in the South Seas, West Indies, India, and Africa. I will recommend you for the West Indies."

"I have given it much thought myself, sir. I wish to continue with my medical studies, under the auspices of the Society, of course. And I feel more doctors are not needed in the West Indies. The Indies are quite civilized. I wish a more primitive land. I wish very much to go to *South Africa*."

"I will convey your wishes to the Board of Directors."

"And I will write them my wishes too, sir."

Rev. Cecil was peeved when he left. He undoubtedly regarded David as an ingrate. But surely the Reverend had forgotten the medical aspect. So David weighed the Reverend's feelings against what David knew was right. He wrote his letter. He wished he was as sure of the rightness of South Africa as he was of the wrongness of the West Indies. Europeans called the continent of Africa the "white man's grave."

The Board approved his request for more medical training. By the beginning of 1840, he moved into London proper and wasted no time rushing to the Aldersgate Street Dispensary. In the office of Doctor Bennett, he said, "I'm David Livingstone, sir. I'm here from the Society."

"Sit down, Livingstone. Forgive me for being abrupt. You'll soon discover in the actual practice of medicine there's little time for normal courtesies. Save them for your patients, who need much reassurance."

"Of course, sir."

The doctor brusquely asked him a number of questions about medicine. Finally, the doctor said, "You have a very sound background in academic medicine. Now you must see real diseases in real people, Livingstone. I'll clear you for Charing Cross Hospital."

For weeks, David spent every working moment with Doctor Bennett. He saw pneumonia, tuberculosis, cancer, and every other disease under the English sun. He began to feel very confident about examining and diagnosing patients. His only regret was the limited resources doctors had to cure patients. They could diagnose diseases well enough. But cures were few and far between.

There were never enough hours in the day for everything

David wanted to do. He began attending lectures of Richard Owen on comparative anatomy. As shy as he was, he forced himself to meet Owen, just as he had forced himself to meet Moffat, and even Mrs. Moffat. Once, he attended a lecture sponsored by the African Civilization Society. Thomas Buxton explained to the audience how only Christianity *and commerce* would change the evil practice of slavery in Africa. If slavery was to be abolished, the powerful African chiefs had to have not only Christianity but a means of providing goods for their people.

It was an unforgettable evening. Prince Albert, the husband of Queen Victoria, was there. And David was struck by the logic of Buxton's message. When someone told him Buxton was advancing the same message as Wilberforce, David felt a pang of guilt as he remembered how he disobeyed his father so many years ago and refused to read the book by Wilberforce.

As the months passed, it became clear where various students were going. Joseph Moore was headed to Tahiti in the South Seas. David's close friend in London, D. G. Watt, was going to India. And David seemed definitely now headed for South Africa—to the very mission run by Robert Moffat. Mrs. Moffat was so convinced David would be miserable without a wife, she promoted an alliance with a woman ten years older than David. He found himself in that awkward situation where his rejection of the match would offend friends. So, with a heavy heart he agreed to meet the woman.

"But I will marry for love or not at all," he told himself.

Before he left for Africa, David returned to Scotland. There he passed the examination for his physician's license. Most important of all, he had to say good-bye to his family. Father Neil was now fifty-two, apparently in good health in the physician's eyes of David. Mother was a concern; she seemed worn out and declining. Brother John was a man of twenty-nine, a merchant like his father. The others seemed to be following David into professions. Brother Charles had immigrated to the United States, where he studied for the ministry at Oberlin College in the state of Ohio. Sister Agnes, sixteen, was preparing for a career in teaching. Sister Janet was already a schoolteacher who loved to write and read poetry. She and David exchanged enthusiastic letters. David could open his heart in letters, as he never could face-to-face. His letters were loquacious, witty, even testy, and more than occasionally blunt.

The visit home to Shuttle Row was spent in discussions by the fire. The Livingstones were optimists. Every new invention and every new discovery would advance the welfare of mankind. Even though they were products of the working class, they did not despise the upper class. Many of the upper class were generous. The grand Bothwell Estate behind Shuttle Row had always kept its grounds open for one and all. The Livingstones prayed the rich could be enlisted in the missionary effort, too.

At five o'clock on the morning of November 17, 1840, they rose to coffee and prayer. Father Neil asked David first to read the 135th Psalm. Then as David read the 121st Psalm, his mother's eyes teared:

> *"I will lift up mine eyes unto the hills, from whence cometh my help. My help cometh from the LORD, which made heaven and earth. He will not suffer thy foot to be moved: he that keepeth thee will not slumber. Behold, he that keepeth Israel shall neither slumber nor sleep. The LORD is thy keeper: the LORD*

*is thy shade upon thy right hand. The sun shall not
smite thee by day, nor the moon by night. The LORD
shall preserve thee from all evil: he shall preserve
thy soul. The LORD shall preserve thy going out and
thy coming in from this time forth, and even for
evermore."*

Tears flowed freely as he parted. Sailing to another continent in 1840 was very risky in itself. And who knew what waited for him in Africa—the "white man's grave"? Once again, Father Neil walked with him into Glasgow—this time to catch the packet steamer to England. All through his youth, his father and mother had guided him on the path of righteousness, encouraging him to study the Bible, encouraging him to go to college, encouraging him in his missionary work, encouraging him to despise slavery. They sent every child to school even though it meant they had to live in poverty. How could David ever thank them? Only by showing them that the effort produced results a hundredfold could he do it. He must do it—for them.

In London, three days later he was ordained Rev. Livingstone along with fellow student William Ross. On December 8, David sailed with Ross and his wife toward Africa on the *George*. Always restless, always eager for opportunity, Livingstone asked Captain Donaldsen to explain the art of navigation to him. The captain was obliging, to the point of showing him how to take lunar observations at midnight with a quadrant. Services on the ship were conducted on Sundays, not by the captain, who was not a Christian, but by David.

"The seamen were sullen and unaffected," David admitted to himself afterwards.

Sailing was arduous. Space was limited. Often during rough

weather, the passengers huddled below in the hold, sick and scared. In midvoyage a mast broke in a storm. Caught in the easterly trade winds and the prevailing easterly currents, the captain navigated the crippled ship across the Atlantic to Rio de Janeiro! David was stunned. Never had he expected to visit the continent of South America. But always ready for opportunity, while the ship was being repaired, he went ashore.

The fact that the Rosses refused to go ashore reinforced his low opinion of them. They had been seasick the entire voyage. David had not been seasick at all, and he doctored them. He knew seasickness was a fickle thing that attacked one person and not another. He felt no superiority at all. But Ross acted as if his manhood was threatened. And Ross had made it clear Livingstone was not to doctor his wife any more.

Ashore, David threw himself headlong into an active mission society, passing out tracts and Bibles to seamen in sleazy waterfront bars. He was spurred by the shame that British sailors were the worst drunks of all. Of course, he was attacked a few times. Few sinners like to be confronted in the act. He even visited hospitals to talk to seamen, some debilitated by alcohol, some stabbed, some beaten.

Only when the *George* was ready to sail again did he return to the ship. On board, his relationship with the Rosses worsened from mutual dislike to mutual scorn. In March 1841, the *George* anchored at Simon's Bay off of Cape Town. The new missionaries were to stay one month at Cape Town before continuing on to their final destination of Port Elizabeth. This time the Rosses came ashore, too. They were all guests of the local station of the London Missionary Society, run by Doctor John Phillips. When David was first alone with Phillips he found himself in a firestorm.

"I suppose Doctor Moffat has told you all about how I

try to dominate all the missions in South Africa," said Phillips defensively.

"I believe, sir, he said you were the financial officer for the Society in South Africa."

"You are being diplomatic, David. Sometimes it's better to be blunt. But I understand you're protecting your benefactor Moffat. Let me tell my side. I have been a staunch and loud protester of slavery. It has decimated my church here. . . ."

"I believe you, sir. I really can't understand why you and Doctor Moffat are not allies."

"He believes I am too political, causing more harm than good by turning the whites against missionaries. He believes all efforts should be spent simply trying to convert the natives to Christianity."

"But what is wrong with that?"

"Wait until you see the frontier yourself, David. Then judge Doctor Moffat's showcase mission."

David *had* heard about Doctor Phillips from Moffat. He expected Phillips to be an ogre. But Phillips was calm and rational, even forgiving. It was obvious to David now that the differences of opinion among missionaries were based on factors more complicated than he yet understood. But he could not sympathize with a missionary who remained in what was already a strong Christian enclave, unless it was because he was campaigning against slavery like Phillips. Some missionaries he met in Cape Town were ministering only to white Christians along the coast, more or less living the soft life of colonists.

Yet deep in his heart, he hoped William Ross and his wife would stay with Doctor Phillips in Cape Town. Phillips had said he needed help. Would the Rosses go to Robert Moffat's mission in Kuruman to forever be thorns in his side?

David LIVINGSTONE

He walked to the pier that morning in April of 1841 when the *George* was to embark, praying it was God's will that the Rosses would not be sailing with him. . . .

FIVE

The Rosses were at the pier, their eyes glacially preoccupied as he approached. David contented himself with the fact that during the voyage he would have pleasant conversations with Captain Donaldsen of the *George*. But the captain sensed his distress as the ship scudded east before the westerlies.

"Cheer up, Livingstone," said the captain. "Next time you disembark—at Port Elizabeth—you will see the real Africa. And certain people who now irritate you will never leave the verandah!"

Several days later, they sailed into Algoa Bay and left the *George*. Livingstone and Ross began procuring supplies. A covered wagon cost fifty pounds. Twelve oxen, each costing three pounds, were required to pull it. Tea, bacon, coffee, cheese, beans, and flour—enough food for three months of travel—would be stowed on the wagon. Cots could be stretched inside the wagon itself at night for sheltered sleeping. Three natives were to be hired to guide them and drive the oxen. The acquisition process was slow. David began to realize that a task that took a few days in Scotland might take several weeks in Africa.

One morning in the hotel where he stayed, he knocked on the door of a room. A red-eyed William Ross opened the door. He pulled a watch from the pocket of his robe. "Good grief, Livingstone, no wonder I'm numb. It's only five o'clock. The sun isn't even up."

"Sorry. But I thought I ought to tell you that while we are waiting for our guides to show up I'm going to visit the mission at Hankey."

"Wait until a decent hour, Livingstone," said Ross, "We'll rent a carriage and make a proper outing of it."

"Excellent. I'll meet you in Hankey." And before Ross could say another word, David was gone. Hankey was thirty miles west along the coastline. He had no wish to spend what little time he had in mounting a proper outing, then dawdling en route to Hankey with the sickly Mrs. Ross. Besides he was going to accompany the missionary from Hankey, who had just arrived in Port Elizabeth and was returning to Hankey. He felt slightly guilty at first, leaving the Rosses behind, but he soon put it out of his mind. He had long been used to weighing the merits of different alternatives, then plunging ahead. He was sure he was living in Christ. The New Testament was full of stories of how Jesus moved ahead, while everyone around Him worried and dallied.

"I want to meet the Hottentots," he told the missionary.

"They are not Hottentots, old boy. That's a white man's name for them. They are the Khoikhoi."

"Do you speak their language?" asked David.

"Hardly, old boy." The missionary laughed.

As they cantered toward Hankey on a sandy wagon trail,

sunbleached Africa dazzled David. To his left stretched beaches of white sand, spattered by azure waves of Jeffrey's Bay. To his right climbed green hills, dotted with mimosa shrubs and runtish acacia trees. Elephants were up there in hidden valleys he was told. What would he do if he saw such a behemoth? It seemed like a dream to be in Africa. It was pleasing beyond anything he imagined.

He heard a musket!

"It's the Khoikhoi," said the missionary.

The Khoikhoi fired welcome shots as they approached. People swarmed around them and shook their hands. Faces were lit with sunny smiles. What a happy mission. David forgave the missionary's comments about the native language when he heard the Khoikhoi speaking. He felt like he was surrounded by crickets. Their speech was punctuated with clicks.

"Can you ever learn it?" asked David, with much more respect.

"They do." The missionary pointed at children playing. "I do understand quite a bit of it myself. But speaking it is very difficult."

"Yes. . ." David was depressed. He wasn't the most distinct speaker anyway, not with his lumpy uvula. "And I thought I was going to learn African."

"Oh, but you can if you want to, old boy. The natives speak Bantu where you are going. I'm not saying it is easy to learn, but it is not as difficult as Nama, the language of the Khoikhoi. You'll probably meet Bushmen north of Kuruman if you ever venture out into the Kalihari wilderness. They also speak Nama."

David sat down in the sun and began writing in a notebook. First of all, the Khoikhoi were not at all like he imagined African natives. Their skin was almost yellow in color. They had high cheekbones and small foreheads. Their black hair coiled tight and flat on their head. And it struck him again how limited his imagination had been. Africa was a treasure. And he had only arrived.

The missionary held a prayer meeting at four o'clock every morning. And many Khoikhoi attended. What a success the mission was enjoying. David's spirits soared.

When he returned to Port Elizabeth, the Rosses were cool. They acted as if they had supervised the entire preparation for the trip in his absence. But David learned they had spent their time strolling past the Regency houses on Cora Terrace, idly wandering though the park created by Sir Rufane Donkin in memory of his wife, and gazing at the walls of Fort Frederick. They had talked of visiting the deserted home of Peter Retief but it was a good two miles away.

"Good riddance, I say," said William Ross.

"This is a much nicer place without the Boers," agreed his wife.

David bit his tongue. Peter Retief had led the Dutch Boers off to the northeast just a few years ago to escape domination by the British. They called themselves *voortrekkers* or pioneers; many were still migrating northeast. The first ones to reach their destination had claimed land held by the Zulus. Now many Zulus were pushed south and west, clashing with the African tribes that held those lands. So two mighty forces were at unrest in the north and east: the Boers and the Zulus. Only a fool would think the English were rid of the problem. God forgive him for thinking such thoughts, but David knew he was looking at two fools.

They began their own trek in the middle of May. It was late fall in southern Africa. Temperatures dropped below 40 degrees at night and peaked at 70 degrees in the afternoon.

Of course, to a Scotsman like David it seemed balmy. The twelve oxen pulled the wagon onto a terrace in the midst of peaks. They were doing well to travel ten miles a day. The Rosses rode in the wagon. David rode the back of an ox. The oxen had horns that swept back behind their heads. He soon learned a bad-tempered ox could knock a man breathless with one quick twist of its neck. But David would risk that, rather than ride with the Rosses. The Rosses slept in the wagon. David pitched a tent and slept on the ground. He made up his mind to keep peace with the Rosses. If he had to avoid them to accomplish that he would. The three were together only when they gathered around a fire every morning and every night to cook a meal.

After one week, they saw in the distance one of their own missions. "Somerset East!" yelled David, from the back of the ox.

A week after Somerset East, they stopped at a mission in Graaf Reinet. It was a small warm town of bright pastels, in spite of being in the shadow of somber pillars eroded from limestone. The town's name seemed to symbolize South Africa to David: Have no fear. They climbed onto yet another terrace among peaks to continue on to a mission at Colesburg. Then they crossed the boulder-bedded Orange River. The wagon hung up on rocks, and the dozen oxen became twisted in their traces so grotesquely, they were pointed the wrong direction. Somehow, they straightened the team out and reached their mission at Phillipolis. The travelers continually rose onto new terraces, reaching new missions. The air grew warmer and drier, the countryside scrubbier. They followed the north bank of the Orange River to a mission at Douglas then crossed the Vaal River to arrive at Griqua Town.

There was much animosity between the mission at

Griqua Town and Moffat's mission in Kuruman. "Moffat takes too much of the credit for missions in South Africa," grumbled one of the missionaries at Griqua Town.

David asked politely, "Isn't Moffat back in England simply trying to raise money?"

"He went back to England because no one in South Africa could publish his translation of the New Testament into the native language of the Bechuanas!" snapped a missionary.

"Didn't Moffat start at this very mission at Griqua Town?" asked David calmly. "Surely. . ."

"He hasn't been here in twenty years! Moffat doesn't like to use native preachers to try to convert the natives," groused one of the other missionaries.

David had to think about that criticism; using native preachers did sound like a very good idea. But he was disappointed. Here was yet another faction among the missionaries of the London Missionary Society. Missionaries in Griqua Town had no love for the missionaries on the coast, either. They considered them slackards. David began to worry. Would there be bickering at Kuruman, too? God forgive him, but he had to look no further than William Ross and his wife to guess the answer to that question.

The land became distinctly flat and arid, occasionally cut by a dry river bed. Trees seemed never at hand, although a few could be seen on the horizon. Yet the land teemed with life, even now in the cool dry season. A traveler had to watch his feet. The ground crawled with snakes, scorpions, spiders, ants, and lizards. Had any white man ever described them before? He had read everything about Africa he could get his hands on. Only one real naturalist had ever worked in South Africa: William Burchell. Burchell had never ventured this far inland. What treasure. Wildebeests, springbucks, and other antelopes flourished in the distance. David suspected a lot of life crept and slithered around his tent after the sun went down, too.

And yet he was troubled. "Where are the Africans?" he would mumble to the back of his plodding ox.

They arrived at Kuruman on July 31, 1841.

Robert Moffat was not there. He was still in England. David and the Rosses were to wait for him to come back to Kuruman. Robert Hamilton was there. And so was Roger Edwards and his wife. Hamilton was in his fifties, Edwards in his late forties, and Ross in his late thirties. David was twenty-eight.

Moffat had built a high-vaulted airy church of adobe. The residences of the missionaries were low buildings with wide eaves and long verandahs. Arranged in a pattern were neat native huts of thatch, circular with cone-shaped roofs. Several hundred natives lived there. Fruit trees and flowering shrubs lent blazes of greenery and color. Vegetables abounded in gardens, fed through irrigation ditches from a magnificent spring called the "Eye of Kuruman." There were a blacksmith shop, a carpentry shed, and several workshops. Nearby was a large corral for cattle. It really was a showcase, just as Doctor Phillips said. Why had he sounded so sarcastic?

David soon learned why. There were over three hundred natives who regularly participated in church. But only forty were communicants. Moffat was not going to allow anyone to water down Christianity. How could David argue with that rigor? And yet he saw Phillips's point now. Moffat had converted forty natives in twenty years—or two per year! And yet he still was adding manpower. For what?

"Where are the Africans?" David would ask himself, when he was alone.

In no time at all, David resolved to push on to the north.

There were far too many missionaries at Kuruman. And hadn't Moffat claimed thousands of natives lived to the north? Within days after his arrival, he confided in a letter to Henry Drummond of Blantyre that he was determined to push on to the north until he found villages of these natives—and furthermore, he intended to be "excluded from all European society." It was not a rash decision. He thought about it all the way from Griqua Town to Kuruman as he wondered: Where are the Africans? And he had given no little thought to being hidden in the shadow of Moffat after meeting Robert Hamilton and Roger Edwards.

Oh, they were kind souls. But how they must have chaffed at the bit over the years. Moffat had used them as artisans, building his showcase. Hamilton was plainly worn out. But Edwards was not.

So David took a chance. "Haven't there been discussions of a mission farther north?" he asked Edwards.

"Oh, of course. It's so obvious, isn't it? Perhaps we can bring it up again before a committee meeting."

"Let us journey north now, Edwards. We'll get a head count of the Africans. What argument could be more powerful for a mission up there? We'll even select a site, if possible. We'll make it easy for the committee."

"Just you and me?"

"Yes."

"You are very bold, Livingstone."

David paused. Was it the iron hand of Moffat that kept his missionaries from venturing north, or was it their own timidity? He continued, "Look at the mission now. Before Ross and I arrived, there were two missionaries here. When you and I leave on our trip north, there will still be two missionaries here."

"It's hard to argue with your simple mathematics," Edwards answered reluctantly.

"If we two do not go, what will we four missionaries do here? Without Moffat, no new work can begin. Surely no one in the Society will begrudge a short trip to the north. It's for the best of purposes."

"I don't know. . ."

"I have a theory, inspired by Moffat himself. After all, Moffat is the one who told me he could look north and see the smoke from a thousand villages. I believe Kuruman is located in an area of nomads. It will never grow much. Farther north there are real settlements of Africans."

"How you talk, Livingstone. Don't tell Robert Moffat that Kuruman won't grow much."

"What if we wait until Moffat gets back to get his permission to reconnoiter and he says no? Or he sends someone else?"

Those possibilities startled Edwards. "You're right. Oh, how I would like to start a new mission of my own."

On September 24, 1841, David left with Roger Edwards and two native Africans who were Christians. David even talked of leaving one of the natives in the north to preach. David had found out from Edwards that Moffat did not object to using native preachers after all. Yes, Moffat had once objected. David began to realize much of the friction among the missionary groups was caused by rumors and lack of communication.

As they journeyed northeast by ox-wagon, he learned from Edwards even more reasons to establish a mission in the north. In the vicinity of Kuruman was a peculiar tribe called Griquas. They were a mix of Khoikhoi and Dutch. They spoke Dutch and used rifles. Many years ago, they had driven the various Bechuana tribes out of the vicinity of Kuruman to the north.

Now Griqua hunters were venturing north among the Bechuana tribes. The Griquas were not only spreading vene- real diseases but lies about the missionaries. It was important for missionaries to get north before the minds of the Bechuana chiefs were permanently poisoned against them.

"But how do you know so much about the tribes to the north if no missionary has been there?" asked David.

"Don't underestimate Moffat. He is fluent in the Sechuana dialect of Bantu. That is the language the Bechuanas speak. He talks to Bechuanas who wander into Kuruman from the north. Don't forget something else: He opened up Namaqualand to the west by bringing the notorious outlaw Afrikaner to Christ. And in the old days before the Boers took over the east, Moffat used to travel to the east, too. He is even a friend of the vicious Zulu chief, Mosilikatze!"

David was heartened by Edward's respect for Moffat. So Moffat was quite shrewd after all. And Moffat knew over twenty years of African history that David was only now learning. David's theory about the area around Kuruman being the realm of nomads was a half truth. The real truth was that the native Bechuana tribes had fled north because of the Griquas. He had so much to learn. And he knew he would never reach the hearts of the Africans unless he learned to speak Bantu dialects like Moffat had done.

The weather was dry and moderate. "Springtime," insisted Edwards.

"Springtime in September." David laughed. "Winter in July. Christmas in the summer. That will take some getting used to."

The country was grassland, flat and scrabbly, scraped by an occasional dry river bed. Locally, the grassland swelled into low brushy hills. Every night, they heard lions and hyenas, sometimes in a frenzy as if they were devouring something. Once in a while at night, the ground thumped from heavy legs. Rhinoceros, speculated David. Too hurried, too confused for elephant. For two weeks, as they traveled during the day they saw only distant antelope in the scrabble and thorn bushes.

David was having doubts. "Where are the Bechuanas, Edwards?"

"Our guides tell me we are very close."

Their two Bechuana guides did not look like the Khoikhoi David had seen at Port Elizabeth. They were darker skinned, taller, and more heavily built. Their features were more like what David expected African natives to look like. The black hair was not coiled as tight and flat as the Khoikhois'. Their cheekbones were more rounded.

His eye caught something on the horizon. "Look, Edwards!"

"I can't see anything."

"It's haze, perhaps smoke from a village."

One of the Bechuana guides named Pomare turned and grinned. *"Ewe!"*

"He said "yes," marveled Edwards as he strained to see ahead.

Soon the scrubby grassland was dotted with rangy, big-boned cattle. And then they saw a herd boy, dressed in a leather robe, carrying a spear. Suddenly, the herd boy darted through the cattle toward what must have been the village. Yes, after a few minutes David saw the conical roofs. Dozens. Then hundreds.

Now as the ox-wagon rumbled past a field of corn, David heard women screaming, *"Luliloo! Luliloo!"*

Men with spears ran from the village to surround their wagon. There seemed to be no animosity. All concerned were overwhelmed with curiosity. David examined their leather robes decorated with beads and some kind of paint, which were worn over leather aprons of the same kind. He puzzled over the strange appearance of their skin. He was sure they were of the same race as their guides but these villagers had apparently smeared grease over their skin. And it had the sheen of metal as if a powdered metal was added to it.

The natives led them to a man who must have been the chief. From his robe of leopard skin dangled tails of lions. His headdress was of some kind of dark fur. The chief was guarded by warriors carrying long spears and gray shields of what must have been rhinoceros or elephant hide.

After a few words between the guides and the chief, which David didn't understand, Edwards gave the chief a string of beads and said in an extremely loud voice, *"Igama lam ngu* Rev. Edwards!" He turned to gesture toward David, "Rev. Livingstone!"

"Igama lam ngu Moseealele," bellowed the chief, even louder than Edwards.

"They are the Bakhatlas," said Edwards to David, never forgetting to smile.

A woman stepped boldly forward and touched David's hair. She tugged it gently and shook her head. Yes, she concluded, David's drab brown thatch must be real hair. She gently pushed the end of his nose. Yes, it was real, too, although it was so much larger than a decent nose should be. In spite of his unease, David could hardly keep from laughing. But that could be fatal. This spoiled woman surely must be a favorite wife of the chief's. Suddenly he felt elated. This was exactly why he came to Africa. These Africans were friendly. They could be reached for Christ. He was sure of it. He felt a smile spread over his face.

"Let me show something," he said. A few murmurs were heard around him. They enjoyed hearing his strange brogue. They, too, were curious. David pointed to his wrist and hand, which were very tan for a Scotsman. He held his hand next to the woman's dark brown arm. "See? My skin is tan. Now see this." He rolled up his sleeve to expose his arm—as pale white as an ostrich egg.

"Hay!" gasped the woman.

The chief was surprised, too, but he motioned the woman to step back. He had indulged her enough. He began talking to the guides. And the guides talked to Edwards. The blood seemed to drain from Edwards's face.

Finally, Edwards spoke with David. "Moseealele wishes to see what we have in the wagon. He is particularly interested in our fire stick."

"Our rifle?"

"Yes, our rifle," said Edwards, forgetting to smile.

SIX

Edwards was pale. His voice trembled. "The chief obviously has heard of firearms. There are Griqua hunters shooting rifles out in the grasslands. The government is very strict about keeping firearms away from natives. I don't believe we should show him. I'll have Pomare tell him we don't have one."

David kept smiling. "But if he finds out later we have a rifle, we'll be forever branded as liars to the Bakhatlas."

"But we know nothing about this chief. Maybe he wants to disarm us before he overpowers us. Other travelers have been murdered."

"I see." David turned and walked through the throng of natives toward the wagon.

"What are you doing, Livingstone?" yelled Edwards.

David reached up under the front seat of the wagon. He turned and two barrels of a very large rifle gaped toward the natives.

"You are going to get us killed!" yelled Edwards.

"It's not loaded." David pointed the barrels at the ground anyway. "I'm just going to show it to the chief."

Edwards's smile was sick. "For goodness' sake, you might have told me what you were going to do before you did it."

"I was too busy praying. We must trust God, Edwards."

David walked up close to Moseealele to show him the rifle. Moseealele examined the weapon very closely. He pulled back the hammers and pulled the triggers. He peered keenly at the rifle. The chief knew far too much about rifles.

"He already has a rifle," said David, smiling vacantly.

"I think you're right," agreed Edwards. "But why such interest? Our rifle is not exactly the latest model."

"I think maybe his rifle is broken. Judging from the fact he's pulled the triggers a dozen times I'll bet it's the trigger mechanism. Ask Pomare to tell him I will fix his rifle for him *after* we return from visiting the tribes farther north."

"But what if you can't fix it?"

"Well, they will probably eat us, Edwards."

"For God's sake, Livingstone. . ."

"Don't forget to smile."

The chief sent one of the warriors to his hut to fetch something. It was his own rifle. David examined it. It was a muzzle loader, even older than David's. The trigger mechanism was broken. "Yes. I'll fix it," he told the chief in very loud voice. And with gestures he showed the chief he knew it was broken, and he could repair it. David noticed Edwards close his eyes as if in prayer.

The missionaries showed other possessions. Of course, these were things that might be used to encourage cooperation from the Bakhatlas later. First they showed them a large mirror. The Bakhatlas went wild over it, passing it around to a constant chorus of laughter. But the missionaries could not make it a gift. They had no more mirrors, and they hoped to visit other villages. The Bakhatlas were respectful of the watch, enjoying the sight of the tiny hand moving, but plainly saw little use for it. Did white men not look at the sun? It was in the sky every day. The chief liked the compass very much, but again why did one need such a thing when the stars in the sky told a man just exactly where to go.

David would not show them the contents of his black doctor's bag. The chief seemed to understand his reticence perfectly. What Bakhatla shaman would show the unknowing his magic wares? And as the word spread that David was a shaman of the whites, there was a groundswell of complaints. Bakhatlas lined up. David insisted on a hut for privacy. He toiled the rest of the afternoon. Most complaints were rheumatism, indigestion, and eye infections. But when one man had a tumor in his leg, David had Pomare tell him that it should be cut out. He assumed the man would scowl in disbelief and leave. But he did not leave. He insisted it be cut out right away. And he sat there stoically talking to another Bakhatla man while David cut into his leg. No one would have guessed the man was seared with pain.

That evening, a cow was to be slaughtered in honor of the missionaries. Fires were already roaring. The missionaries watched. One of the warriors speared the animal deftly in the heart. There was hardly a visible wound. The animal barely stopped kicking when warriors leaped in to butcher it. Apparently, the butchers were entitled to the blood and the heart. Chunks of meat were sliced up and distributed. Their recipients immediately threw them on the fire.

David noticed even Pomare was wide-eyed. "Ask him why he is so excited, Edwards."

After an earnest conversation, Edwards said dryly, "He

says when you have eaten rhinoceros you will understand."

"What a wonderful sense of humor!"

Things could hardly have been better. David estimated there were two thousand of these Bakhatlas. But he had more appreciation for what Moffat had done. He could see a missionary could not hope to reach the Bakhatlas with the message of Christ without knowing their dialect of Bantu. Learning their language would have to become a top priority for him.

That night they were honored by sleeping in a hut. Edwards stopped abruptly in the entrance and sniffed long and hard. "Always smell before you enter, Livingstone. If you smell something acrid, get out!"

"What does it mean?"

"It means you've frightened a snake inside the hut. The smell is from some dreadful thing it excretes."

"I've seen very few snakes in Africa so far."

"They are plentiful but camouflaged. There is one that's not camouflaged. It's long and black. Don't walk. Don't run. Fly. It's the *mamba*. You will not survive its bite."

They entered the hut and slept on mats of woven rushes. But they discovered the next morning that they shared the hut with creatures that came out at night. Wedged between their toes and fingers were dozens of dark blue orbs.

"Tampan," said Edwards in disgust.

"What are they?"

"Ticks. Don't pull them out. Their heads will remain under your skin. Let's try alcohol. Then we'll toast them."

Bathed in alcohol, then heated by the glowing end of a burning stick, the blood-swollen ticks gradually pulled their heads out to look for a more hospitable host. Edwards didn't seem pleased with their withdrawal. David said, "Smile, Edwards. We've almost got all of them out."

"Oh, the nasty part is yet to come."

"My hands and feet do feel rather numb."

"That's not nasty enough, Livingstone. Either one of two things will happen to you next. You'll feel perfectly all right but get a terrible fever in a day or two. Or you'll soon become violently sick. . ."

"Are you sure? Why don't we have these pests at Kuruman?"

"We cover the floors with a mud plaster. These vermin live in the soil."

"Oh!" David felt an overpowering urge to throw up. He scrambled out the low door of the hut into the morning sun. He never got off his hands and knees.

"Smile, Livingstone," called Edwards with a vengeance.

But Edwards was soon beside him. After a long time, they stood up on rubber legs.

"Thank the Lord, that's over," said David in a weak voice.

"If it were only true," commented Edwards dryly.

"What do you mean? I feel. . ." Suddenly he was struck by another illness: diarrhea.

Later, they burned an area of the ground away from the huts and covered it with a tarpaulin. Then they pitched their tent, where they intended to sleep for the duration. David explained to the chief that his medicine worked better there. And it certainly did for him. Dozens of Bakhatlas were gathered around their tent all day, waiting to see the white shaman.

Over the next few days, David and Edwards learned much about the customs of the Bakhatlas through hand gestures and help from their two guides. Someday, the chief would pass his authority on to the oldest son of his favorite wife. The chief had many wives. Often a chief was a chief simply because he had many wives who had many children.

The Bakhatlas made iron but they were not yet going to

show these outsiders how they did it. Both men and women wore leathers and furs, which were hunted, tanned, and even sewn by the men. The women tended the corn, built huts, prepared food, gathered firewood, and hauled water.

"How I hate to leave these wonderful people," said David as he and Edwards climbed into the wagon.

But leave they did. Pomare and the other guide now directed them to the northwest. This time, David was aware of where they were going. To the Bakwains.

At one point, a small bird harassed the wagon. It would swoop in and flit away, then return to do the same thing. "What is it?" asked Edwards of Pomare.

Pomare grinned and pretended to be eating something scrumptious. He spoke a few words in Sechuana.

Edwards shook his head. "He says the bird is inviting you to come with him to find something very delicious."

"I must see this." David leaped down from the wagon.

"For goodness' sake, Livingstone, there are lions in this area. Especially in the brush of those low hills."

But the low hills were exactly where David was headed. He had a low opinion of lions. He didn't tell Edwards because he didn't want to worry him but he had already come across lions when he strolled away from the wagon in the evenings. As long as one didn't surprise a lion and as long as one showed no fear, the lion would give a long hard look and then slowly walk away. So David fearlessly followed the bird but he looked well ahead for any tawny shapes lying among the bushes.

"So this is your prize," said David as the bird flitted around a grotesque baobab tree well in front of the hills. The tree had a massive trunk with spindly branches. In a crotch of the tree was a dark mass swarming with bees. "You must be the African honey guide I read about. I thought it was a fable. So it's true. Oh, Africa, you are marvelous."

He thought about John the Baptist in the wilderness. Hadn't David seen locusts off and on for days? How could one pass up such an opportunity? He collected some of the honey, making sure his feathery guide got its share, and walked back to the wagon. Later that afternoon, they ran across a cluster of locusts. He collected some of them. He wrote notes in his diary.

"You take notes about everything, don't you?" Edwards remarked.

"Nearly so."

"And now you're describing locusts?"

"Yes."

That night he pounded the locusts into a paste and mixed it with honey. He offered Edwards a spoonful. "Care for some?"

"Is that concoction what I think it is, Livingstone?"

"Yes. Matthew, chapter three, verse four."

"Since you put it that way I can scarcely refuse."

David tasted it, too. "Rather shrimpy. Quite good."

"Treat yourself to the rest of my share," said Edwards dryly. "I'm a Luke, chapter 15, verse 23 man myself."

"The fattened calf?" David chuckled. How he loved this life!

Only four days from the Bakhatlas they saw cattle, then another village. Were they reaching denser and denser populations? David could hardly restrain his optimism. And once again a herd boy sounded the alarm. Their greeting was just like the previous meeting: alarm, suspicion, curiosity, appreciation for their gifts of trinkets, then fascination with their possessions—especially the mirror. The chief of these Bakwains was Sechele, a man of about thirty-five. He struck David as being particularly friendly and quick-witted.

The missionaries stayed several days, this time refusing the hospitality of a hut by explaining ahead of time David could work his medicine only out of his own tent. The Bakwains seemed very much like the Bakhatlas, but David cautioned himself not to jump to conclusions just because they dressed alike and lived in similar huts.

"What is the quickest route back to Kuruman?" asked Edwards after several days. He was already assuming David would know. After all, every step of the journey David seemed to be studying his compass then scribbling observations and small maps in his note book.

"We must go back to the Bakhatlas."

"But isn't that out of our way?" asked Edwards.

"I promised to fix Chief Moseealele's rifle."

"It's not too soon then for me to start praying."

They returned by the same route. Moseealele greeted them like old friends. And much to Edward's relief, David managed to repair the trigger mechanism on Moseealele's old musket. Once again, dozens of Bakhatlas lined up to see the white shaman. But David had to be firm. He and Edwards would be there indefinitely if he stayed to doctor all of them. He promised Moseealele he would return. The chief was pleased. After all, David had kept his promise to return before. Here was man who could be trusted.

"Always make them a promise you can keep," said David their first night away from the Bakhatlas.

"Good grief, Livingstone, you're as cunning a fox as Robert Moffat himself."

Suddenly, a young African girl wandered into their camp. Pomare spoke to her. Then he spoke to Edwards.

Edwards sighed. "The girl has run away from the Bak-hatlas to seek our protection. She was orphaned recently when her sister died. The Bakhatlas are going to sell her to the highest bidder. She is loaded with beads because they have decorated her to make her more attractive. Shall we take her back to the village?"

Before David could answer Edwards, a warrior approached. He was angry, obviously pursuing, now demanding the girl. To David's surprise, Pomare stepped forward and refused to give up the girl. Did Pomare know how to handle the situation? David reached for his rifle. Pomare stripped the girl of her beads and gave them to the warrior. The warrior nodded happily. The crisis was over. The beads were very precious to the Bakhatlas.

They were back in Kuruman by Christmas. Moffat was still not there. That made Edwards feel better about their rash trip north. Not much had happened at the mission. It was now the hottest and wettest time of the year. David was inundated by the natives for medical treatment at the mission, too. He excised tumors, cured eye infections, and gave tablets for indigestion. He was very skilled at diagnosing ailments. And even if he could not cure every patient, many found comfort in knowing their disease was not going to be fatal. His treatments were limited. But the natives thought he was a wizard.

David had a burning desire to go north again. He was convinced beyond all doubt that the Bechuana tribes would never receive the gospel from a missionary unless the missionary spoke their tongue. This time, Edwards was not willing to go with him. He had seen enough. So in February of 1842, David went north again with Pomare and another guide. Never one to miss an opportunity he took a different route to the Bakwains, making observations and maps all the way. Before he arrived at the location where he was certain to find Sechele and his Bakwains, he found another village!

"What is this place?" he asked his guides in his limited Bantu.

"The village of Chief Bubi of the Bakwains."

For the first time, David knew the Bakwains had two chiefs. Bubi welcomed him.

Over the next few days, David discerned that Sechele and Bubi were bitter enemies. Years ago when Sechele was a child and the tribe was still whole, Bubi and another man named Molese had murdered the chief, who was Sechele's father. The child Sechele was secreted away far to the north to live with a very great Makalolo chief named Sebitoane. The two murderers split the tribe. Years later, Sechele returned to defeat Molese. But the tribe was still split. And now David was in the village of Sechele's enemy, Bubi.

David picked up Bantu very fast. He was not doctoring all the time. After he learned that every chief also had the responsibility of making rain, he told the Bakwains he too could make rain. The natives were astonished to see the white shaman digging earth like an anteater tearing into an anthill. What was he doing?

David believed the other missionaries were too polite, always asking permission to do things. Too often the chief would show his authority by refusing. If David just went ahead and did it, the natives could judge for themselves if it would benefit them. As soon as they realized he was a making a canal from the river to their field of corn, they too were digging like anteaters. What a celebration they had when precious water rushed through the canal to their thirsty corn!

David was soon preaching in the native dialect. "Praise the Lord! He has given His blood for your sins. God so loved the world that He gave His one and only son."

As David sermonized more and more, he uncovered

more and more difficulties. The word he was using for love was used by the Bakwains for sexual love. The word he was using for sin meant cow dung if he said it in the wrong pitch. Bantu was a tonal language. The same word could mean several radically different things, depending on the pitch. But still he had to start his gospel. He had to let them know the real reason he was there. He had to save their souls. Now he was realizing how difficult that would be. Every day he appreciated Robert Moffat's accomplishments more.

After a few weeks David pushed on, accompanied by Bakwain warriors. If larger villages were to the north, he had to know. But the hill-dotted plain became too sandy for his ox-wagon. The oxen were taken out of harness and loaded with supplies. The trekkers proceeded on foot. Often David would ride an ox.

Two weeks later, he entered the village of the Bamangwatos. Chief Sekomi informed him that three thousand Bamangwatos lived in the village. When the natives began calling David "God" after he doctored them, he realized again what a task awaited him in explaining the gospel. Their god was far too small.

"Be careful. We have many lions here," warned Sekomi.

David suspected the chief did not want him poking around the village too much. One morning very near where he camped, he heard the most heartrending cries of children. The wailing went on the entire day. A lion had jumped their mother right on the outskirts of the village and had eaten her. But David still did not fear lions. On the trail, he had seen lions approach his oxen at night. As long as the oxen held their ground the lion would not attack. But if an ox panicked and ran, the lion would attack it immediately. Surely the poor woman had seen the lion and made the fatal mistake of not standing her ground.

David learned something about the nature of men, too. One night, Sekomi came to his tent privately and said, "I wish I could change my heart. It is always proud and restless. I am always very angry with my people. Give me medicine to change my heart."

David held up the Bible. "This is the only medicine that can change your heart."

"No! I want my heart changed at once. Give me some medicine to drink."

When David would produce no magic elixir, Sekomi left his tent. After a few weeks of working with the Bamangwatos, David told Sekomi that he was going to venture farther north. Sekomi warned David about the Bakaas to the north. They were treacherous. They murdered travelers. He should not go. There were tales that the Bakaas had seen white men before, traders from the east. The Bakaas did not fear white men; neither did they like them.

When David insisted on going, Sekomi sent four warriors with him. They were to accompany him all the way north, then all the way south on his return trip to Kuruman. Of course David realized their presence was more than protection. The chief wanted information about what all his neighbors were doing. David now had a contingent of Bakwains and Bamangwatos.

Many days farther north, he encountered the Bakaa village. This time there was no welcome, no happy sharing of mirrors and beads. All the village seemed deserted except the chief and his attendants, who simply stood and stared belligerently.

"The chief refuses to offer you food," whispered Pomare. "That is a very bad sign."

"And where are the other Bakaas?" whispered David.

Were the other Bakaas quietly flanking David and his escort? Was this a trap? Was this the end?

SEVEN

For the benefit of those in his own party, David said, "My God will keep us safe. You'll see."

David said a silent prayer. He really did put his trust in God. If God wanted him to bring the gospel to Africa, God would protect him. David coolly prepared his own corn-meal mush, ate it, and then stretched out to nap right in front of the Bakaa chief. What were these Bakaas to make of such trust in this white man?

Finally, with a great sigh of relief, Pomare said, "They are preparing food. They are going to welcome us."

Later, David talked the Bakaas into assembling for a sermon. He climbed a rocky hillside and spoke to them below. He was becoming more skilled at avoiding linguistic pitfalls. But he never knew for sure how the natives interpreted his sermon until they asked him questions afterward. That was very important in his own growth.

He slipped on the way off the rocks and broke his finger. With his friend Sehamy's help, he set the finger with a reed splint. He didn't stay with the Bakaas long. He had already been away from Kuruman several months. And when he left the village to venture farther north, the Bakaa chief sent yet more warriors to escort him.

As they left the village, David overheard the Bakaa warriors speaking in Bantu. One said, "This white man is not strong. He is skinny. He only appears to be stout because he puts on baggy clothes. He will soon break down like an old woman."

From that moment, David needed no prodding to maintain a murderous pace. By the time they reached the next village to the north, the village of the Makalakas, his detractors were too exhausted to insult him. The Makalakas were a small tribe. And they were the first tribe he encountered that wasn't like the others farther south. They were darker skinned, spoke a different dialect, and planted their corn on ridges. Pomare told David they were on the fringe of another realm, that of the great Makalolo chief Sebitoane. David had gone far enough this time. He and his escorts headed back to Kuruman.

One night on the trek back, lions roared right next to the camp, trying to stampede the oxen. David grabbed a pistol he kept by his side at night and fired into the darkness. He was racked with pain. When he examined his hand by the light of the campfire he saw the recoil had reinjured his broken finger so violently it was bleeding. He knew he could show no pain because the natives themselves acted oblivious to pain. So he sat stoically as Sehamy tried to straighten his mangled finger and tie it in a splint.

"It was good only lions were out there," said Sehamy philosophically. "A rhinoceros will charge right into a fire at night."

David had a lot of time to think on the journey back.

Over the weeks he had heard more and more, not only about the Makalolo chief to the north, Sebitoane, but a Zulu chief to the east, that dreaded Mosilikatze. Only the great Sebitoane to the north could stand up to Mosilikatze. Every other tribe was helpless against his onslaught. On his way back David reflected that the desire of all the chiefs to have him come and live with them might not be because they desired the gospel but because they hoped Mosilikatze would not attack a village with a white shaman.

David arrived at Kuruman at the end of June 1843. In five months, he had changed. He was lean and battered, but very confident. He spoke a reasonable amount of Bantu. The misionaries at Kuruman had never seen anyone like him. He was fearless in the wilderness. David assured them that if one was careful with dangerous animals like the lion, rhinoceros, elephant, crocodile, and leopard, one would just have to be very unlucky to get hurt.

"I don't intend to find out," muttered William Ross.

Only Edwards seemed to understand him.

Moffat was still not back from England. So what choice did David have? He doctored the natives at Kuruman through one more hot summer and then left in February of 1843 on another trip. He couldn't waste the valuable cold dry season, the only season really suitable for traveling. Again, he and his guides were alone. David had already heard that Sechele was very angry with him for visiting his rival Bubi. Messengers from Sechele made it clear that the missionary David was no longer welcome.

So naturally David told Pomare, "We shall proceed immediately to the village of Sechele."

When David's wagon arrived at the Bakwain village, Sechele was very agitated. But his agitation had nothing to do with David. Sechele's son was very sick. And the son of one of his best warriors was even sicker, emaciated from dysentery. David began doctoring the boys immediately. Any sickness, especially with fever, was feared with dread. Anyone in the wilderness could appear completely healthy one week and be stone dead from a fever the next week.

David had just learned that the Bakwain Sehamy, his resourceful helper from the previous trip, had recently died from fever. It broke David's heart to wonder if he had brought Sehamy to Christ.

"Poor Sehamy," he cried. "Where are you now? I told you about Christ. Did you think of Him when you were dying? Did He lead you through the dark valley?" It was so awful to think of souls lost to eternity. That goaded David on his crusade at all times.

He doctored the two boys back to health. Sechele was now a great friend. And Sechele was a fountain of information about Africa. David had already heard of the legendary place west of the realm of Sebitoane called Lake Ngami. It was supposedly paradise right in the middle of the wilderness. One could not reach it by skirting the arid Kalahari wilderness to the east because of Mosilikatze. And one could not cross the Kalahari itself unless the previous season had been exceptionally rainy, warned Sechele, so that one could find plenty of the small striped melons for water.

"And even then one must avoid the dreaded tsetse fly," added Sechele, who proceeded to tell David everything he knew about the pest.

The tsetse fly was a small fly that looked like a bee. It lived north of the Bakaas in wooded areas. It was harmless to all wild game and humans. And yet, no domestic animals except donkeys were safe from it. Oxen, cattle, goats, hogs, horses, and dogs were not safe. Death could be within days or months. But the animal was almost certain to weaken and die. The distribution of the flies was very uneven. One could cross open grassland between wooded areas and be in or out of tsetse country. One might leave a wooded area infested with tsetse flies by crossing a river and enter a wooded area free of the flies. Tsetse flies had contributed heavily to the white man's dread of Africa. After all, how could a white man survive without his stock?

When David returned to Kuruman, Edwards greeted him. "I have permission to start a new mission station in the north," said Edwards. And he added dryly, "With you, of course."

"Praise the Lord," said David.

Moffat was still not back from England. And that night David thanked God he had not waited. He had been in South Africa for over two years already. He and Edwards proceeded immediately to a location near the Bakhatlas. They signed a formal agreement with Moseealele and his Bakhatlas in August of 1843. They would call the mission Mabotsa. A mission building of fifty feet by eighteen feet was begun, under the skilled hands of Edwards. For all his lack of imagination, Edwards was now the driving force of the mission. He was the artisan. He knew how to set up the physical part of a mission.

"And a fine mission it will be, too," enthused Edwards.

"It is better located than Kuruman," said David. "We have abundant water and wood. It will be better than Kuruman."

"Easy, Livingstone," said Edwards nervously.

Mabotsa was next to wooded hills. The Bakhatlas mined iron ore out of the hills and smelted it. The area had one drawback. The hills were a refuge for countless lions, which preyed on their cattle so boldly they attacked even in daylight. The Bakhatlas had suffered so much from lions, they had become submissive, as if it were their destiny to suffer lions. The Bakhatlas were bewitched.

David encouraged them to confront lions as other tribes did. Warriors of other tribes circled their quarry, always tightening the circle. When close, the warriors would hurl dozens of spears into the beast.

But lions continued to prey on their cattle. David himself had no fear of lions. Yet he was not foolish enough to volunteer his services. His whole experience had been in avoiding fights with lions. Hunting lions was far different. Lions would fight to the death if attacked. And when one man stood alone with one double-barreled rifle that took far too long to reload, the lion had a very good chance of bringing the man down if he missed or the gun misfired. No, he could only encourage the Bakhatla warriors to have the gumption to take care of the lions themselves.

In December, David learned Robert Moffat had finally disembarked at Port Elizabeth and was on his way up the trail to Kuruman. In January, David impulsively jumped on a horse to ride from Mabotsa to meet the Moffats as they crossed the Vaal River 150 miles away.

"Good grief. Livingstone?" cried Robert Moffat, not completely approving.

"Yes, sir. I wanted to see you."

Moffat showed David a copy of his freshly printed New Testament in the Sechuana dialect. And David saw Moffat's daughters for the first time. Bessie was a teenager, far too young to interest thirty-year-old David, now a weathered outdoorsman. Ann was older but still too young. But Mary was twenty-two. She was not plump but stout. Dark brown hair parted in the middle and pulled severely behind into a bun framed a triangular face as tan as David's. Her nose was long and sharp. By any standard, she was not beautiful. But how alive her face was! David was startled at the warmth coming from her dark eyes. She was no coquette but full of life. And she plainly saw no reason not to let David know she found him very agreeable.

"It's always better to be straightforward," he said to her in a careless moment.

Was Mary the real reason he had ridden madly over the wilderness to meet Robert Moffat? Was it God's guiding hand that put the idea in his head? Because now that he was there, he felt very foolish in the eyes of Robert Moffat. His trips to the north were based on sound reasons. But what a wild thing this trip was!

By the time David had accompanied the Moffats to Kuruman, he knew Mary quite well. She, too, was forward, a bit wild in her thinking. Her parents' disapproval of David's impulsiveness had only sharpened her interest in him. Mary even spoke Bantu—with no accent at all. After all, she had been born in Griqua Town and raised in South Africa. When they saw a giraffe, she called it a *tootlooa* as naturally as breathing. An anteater was *takaru*, a rabbit *tlolo*. Was David wrong in his resolution never to have a wife? He had only considered an English wife, a woman alien to Africa, a woman constantly wistful and unhappy in Africa. How narrow his thinking had been.

While David rode back to Mabotsa in confusion, he became sure of one thing. "I'll write dear Mary!" he cried, startling gemsbok antelopes into springing across the plain.

After he returned to Mabotsa, he did write her. He was very busy now. Edwards and his wife were cooler to him now.

David's trip had not set well. He was sure Edwards felt he was once again being treated only as an artisan. Edwards wanted to be treated as an equal. He did not want to be dominated again like Robert Moffat had dominated him. David tried to assure him he was an equal. But Edwards was put off by his aggressiveness. And David understood whereas Edwards once bowed to David's domineering ways, he could not bow to David in the presence of his wife.

"Perhaps you can help the Bakhatlas," said Edwards dryly. "They are having more trouble than ever with the lions."

So one day, David rallied them into doing something about it. Spears in hands, the warriors trudged toward a wooded hill they knew was a favorite with the marauders. To encourage them, David promised to back them up. He took the double-barreled rifle. And Mebalwe, a native teacher he was training, also carried a rifle. Together, they stayed on the plain and watched the spectacle, rifles ready.

Sure enough, the warriors trudged up the hill, catching a huge black-maned male in their tightening circle. But the lion broke through. That shouldn't have been possible if the warriors had stood their ground. But their hearts were not in it. They were bewitched. David shook his head and walked back to the mission.

Suddenly Mebalwe pointed. *"Tau."*

"Lion?" whispered David. "Where?"

Then he saw the huge black-maned lion. It was crouched behind a bush, tail rigid. David had seen that crouch, that rigid tail before; those signs were a prelude to certain attack. A lion could hit top speed almost immediately. A victim would be hit by five hundred pounds of lion going forty miles an hour. This lion crouched no more than two seconds away.

David cocked both hammers of the rifle and fired both

barrels into the bush. The bullets were half-ounce slugs. The lion didn't flinch.

Bakhatlas were dancing all around now, screaming in Sechuana, "He's shot! He's shot!"

"Don't anyone approach him," yelled David. "I want to reload."

He put a packet of powder in the gun and began to ram the bullets down the muzzle of the barrel. Suddenly, he heard screams. It was the lion! The great jaws snapped on his left arm. He was bowled to the ground. The lion shook him. David felt numb. So this was the end. He watched the lion gnashing on the sleeve of his jacket. He felt no fear, no alarm, no regret. The dreamy stupor was surely God's mercy to any poor unfortunate in such circumstances, man and animal alike. He remembered the agony from his broken finger. He felt nothing now. He moved his head from under a huge hot paw. The teeth were no longer grinding. The large yellow eyes were intent on something else. David heard an explosion. Suddenly, the lion bolted away from him!

He rolled over to see the lion mauling a native. A rifle went flying. "Oh no," cried David. "Not faithful Mebalwe."

Suddenly, one of the Bakhatlas was jamming a spear into the lion. The lion abandoned Mebalwe to attack his new attacker. The lion seized his shoulder, then spun and fell dead. Praise the Lord. David watched Mebalwe trying to rise. His leg was covered with blood. The other Bakhatla was bloody but alive, too. Praise the Lord.

David could barely feel the Bakhatlas carrying him in a litter to the mission. He tried to regain his senses as he was placed on a mat in his hut. He realized Edwards and his wife were standing over him.

"We killed a lion," explained David. "We botched it badly."

"Livingstone," gasped Edwards. The face of his wife was white as snow. David knew he must look a bloody mess.

"Wash out the wound first," David instructed Edwards. "Lion bites give terrible infections. You'll just have to do as I say."

"Doesn't he always?" muttered Mrs. Edwards as she stumbled out of the hut.

"You'll have to feel my arm to see how badly fractured the humerus is," said David as Edwards washed the blood away. "But first, what is the damage to the muscle?"

Edwards winced as he examined the wounds. "I count eleven punctures."

"Could have been worse. Pray I don't get infection."

"Now I'm going to feel the bone, Livingstone. Hang on." And Edwards kneaded the arm like bread. "It's completely broken. It's as if you have another joint."

"You're going to have to set it in a splint."

Soon David had a very rigid splint on his arm. Edwards did a good job. David had instructed him every step of the way. Mrs. Edwards returned to say, "Mebalwe's thigh is cut badly, but the bone is not broken. The other man's injuries are even lighter."

"Each one suffered less in the teeth of the dying lion," said David. "The other Bakhatla is the one I rescued after he was gored by a buffalo. Very nice of him to return the favor. By the way, Mrs. Edwards, if you're ever attacked by a buffalo, lie flat and grab hold of the grass. The brute can't get his horn under you that way and toss you in the air."

"I'll remember that," she sobbed.

"Relax, Livingstone," said Edwards. "There's nothing more you can do now."

"Get some rest yourself, Edwards. And let's not make a big

thing out of this. I'm not exactly proud of bungling the affair."

At last David could relax. But in his physician's head he knew relaxation was an illusion. The body's natural pain killers would wear off. And excruciating pain would begin to throb. *Oh God, if this is Your will,* he prayed, *I accept it. Give me the strength I know You can give.*

David fought the pain day after day, always reminding himself to be grateful to God. Yes, he was alive. God had other things for him to do yet. This pain was nothing. This pain was not permanent. It would go away. He didn't even get a bad infection like Mebalwe and the other man got. His jacket must have wiped the filth off the fangs as they penetrated his arm.

As David began to feel better, Mrs. Edwards could not resist asking, "What went through your mind while the lion had your arm? Did you have visions of glory?"

"I wondered what part of me the lion would eat first," answered David in gruesome candor.

David was an invalid for two months. He knew the mending humerus was fragile. Any activity might give him a permanently useless arm. He had a lot of time to think. It was not time wasted. He thought of how terribly difficult it was to convert the Bakhatlas to Christ, even with native teachers. He thought of the most intelligent, most pliable native he had met so far: Sechele. If one could convert a chief like Sechele, wouldn't the rest of the Bakwains quickly follow? He realized now that he and Edwards had picked the right location—but the wrong tribe. They should have connected their mission to Sechele's Bakwains. It was not too late. In fact, it was a solution. Edwards was not happy with David's impulsive acts. So why couldn't David move on to open up yet another mission farther north?

That would be a primary objective. But first, he had something else equally important to do.

Edwards spotted him preparing to leave. "Let me see, Livingstone. Are you saddling the horse or harnessing the oxen? Oh, I see you're saddling the horse, so I guess you're going to ride madly south to Kuruman."

"See that you give Roger his proper due to Mister Moffat," said Mrs. Edwards brashly. "You needn't take all the credit."

"If such a thing were possible I would not talk to Robert Moffat at all on this trip," answered David. And he spurred the horse south.

EIGHT

When David returned to Mabotsa he told Edwards and his wife, "Mary Moffat and I are engaged. We are to be married in Kuruman this coming January."

"Really?" said Edwards unenthusiastically.

Always pushing himself to the limit, David rebroke his arm handling adobe bricks for the mission building. The break formed a false joint now. When he lifted his left arm the humerus bent. He could no longer lift his left arm above shoulder level. Did that mean he could no longer shoot a rifle? He had to know.

"I couldn't hit an elephant from ten yards," he told himself after shooting at a target. He could no longer hold the heavy rifle steady with his left arm.

He shrugged off the inconvenience and learned to sight with his left eye, steadying the rifle with his right arm and pulling the trigger with his left. Soon he could shoot nearly as well as he ever shot. It was no small triumph, not to someone who craved the wilderness like David.

When he returned to Mabotsa with his bride Mary in January of 1845, she was regarded by Edwards as an extension of Robert Moffat. Edwards could not speak his mind; he felt once again under Moffat's thumb. So David's relationship with Edwards worsened. Edwards was now threatening to write letters about David's overbearing behavior. So fiery David wrote a long letter to the London Missionary Society defending himself. Then Edwards did not send his letter, making David look very thin-skinned.

Yet David felt he had no special influence with Moffat. His suggestion for a seminary for natives was roundly scorned by the missionaries at Kuruman, who now made all decisions by committee. And David was more and more disillusioned with the Bakwains, who trudged halfheartedly to sermons but steadfastly rejected the gospel. The only lights in his life were God and his marriage to Mary. She was as bold as David.

Mary said, "You've told me a hundred times you don't care where we go as long as it's *forward*."

"But the committee will not fund a new location."

"Are we slaves to money?"

Early in 1846, the Livingstones had an infant: Robert. And David had left Mabotsa for a new location farther north: Chonuane. He had to dip into his own meager salary of one hundred pounds a year to finance the buildings, but both he and Mary thought it was worth every penny to get away from Edwards. And the Bakwains seemed intractable in their heathen beliefs.

"On the other hand, Sechele is very cooperative," enthused David.

Sechele was a true prodigy. David started him on Robert Moffat's translation of the Old Testament into the Sechuana dialect. Within two days, Sechele had mastered the alphabet.

Within weeks he was reading; Isaiah was his favorite book. David was startled by Sechele's new thirst for anything English. The chief began buying and wearing English clothes. On a particular day, he wore whatever caught his fancy. It was not unusual to see Sechele wearing a red hunting cap and a red blazer over his leather apron.

One very hot day, Mary said to David, "Did you see what Sechele is wearing today? A bulky Mackintosh coat and wading boots."

David, who always wore a gold-banded blue cap with a stiff bill, replied, "Just so he doesn't get one of those dreadful white safari helmets."

David's success with Sechele, who now began truly to understand the meaning of Christ, offset the disappointment in Chonuane as a location. Selected in haste, it appeared lush but actually suffered from lack of water. And despite knowing what the missionaries at Kuruman would say, David abandoned it and the investment of his meager salary to move forty miles further into the wilderness by the river Kolobeng. The new mission, called Kolobeng, was started August 1847. When Mary arrived with Robert and a second infant, Agnes, she saw herds of buffaloes and zebras. Kolobeng seemed an oasis along a river that drained wooded hills all around.

One of David's next goals was to convince Sechele his five wives were four wives too many. Sechele was anxious to cooperate, but the wife problem was very difficult. A chief simply didn't shed his wives. It disgraced them and their families. It seemed inhuman even to David. But Sechele nevertheless tried, even though it undermined his authority as chief.

Another of David's goals was to place native teachers into the lands far to the east of Kolobeng. Always eager to travel he made several trips east. The eastern lands were now settled and controlled by the Dutch Boers. It had been less than fifty years since the English had landed troops in the Cape region. It had been less than fifteen years since the English banned slavery in South Africa. It had been less than ten years that most of the Boers settled in the lands east of Kolobeng. They despised the British.

When David returned from his last eastern trip, Mary asked, "Were the Boers receptive to a mission this time?"

If only he could spare Mary. But she would want no secrets. And besides, she was far too shrewd about African ways. "Quite the opposite," he answered.

"Quite quite?"

"Yes. Hostile would be the appropriate word."

"They don't fear your missions in the east, David. They fear that you will push north. The farther north you push, David, the more the Boers will oppose you. They are afraid you will open up the north to traders, then merchants, then farmers, and then the English will flood into an area now closed to them."

"If only I could introduce trade into the north."

"Perhaps that is the answer."

"To spreading the gospel? Yes, I agree with that view more and more. A man named Wilberforce used to say that. Now Buxton says the same thing. Christianity must be spread in Africa by opening the heathen areas to commerce, too."

"It might also be the answer to preventing the Boers from moving into that area."

"Yes." He frowned. "If Boers ever control the north country I would never be able to push north."

"You are making wonderful progress with Sechele," she said.

"But the other Bakwains are not earnest in their interest in the gospel. Even Sechele is amazed by their indifference. For seventeen years, they have imitated their chief's every whim. But in loving the gospel, Sechele is an anathema to them. I should be doing so much more," he lamented.

"What happened to your desire to push north?" she asked.

"No funds. Sound familiar?"

"What would excite the interest of the outside world?"

"Why, the legendary Lake Ngami, of course. Yes, that would certainly raise interest in the area if such a place could be found. . ."

". . .by you?"

"Perhaps one of the recreational hunters would finance a trip. Not for my reasons, of course. But what hunter can resist an area that has never been hunted before?"

"They have resisted the temptation up until now."

David laughed. "You keep pulling me back and forth, Mary. Are you two steps or three steps ahead of me?"

"Well, why haven't the hunters gone north?"

"The natives are too dangerous. Mosilikatze is in the northeast. And Sebitoane is in the north. Not to mention the Bakaas in between."

"But you know the chiefs, don't you?"

"Oh, Mary, all right. But how can I leave you and the children all the time?"

"I know why you are doing it. Do you think my wish to spread the gospel of Jesus Christ is any less than yours? I'm a child of missionaries."

So David, who was a prodigious writer of letters, added Captain Thomas Steele to his long list of correspondents. He first met Steele in the early days of Mabotsa. Steele was exemplary in dealing with natives. He seemed more like a philosopher than a hunter. It was clearly the lure of the exotic countryside that made him hunt.

By the time David's trip north firmed up, Mary had given birth to their third child: Thomas Steele Livingstone. But Steele was not to go with David. He had recommended as his replacement an equally civil hunter named Cotton Oswell. David had met Oswell several years earlier. Oswell was wealthy, classically educated, and totally devoid of personal ambition. Oswell invited his friend Mungo. And yes, the two recreational hunters would finance the entire trip.

When the two hunters arrived in Kolobeng, Oswell informed· David, "We have twenty horses, eighty oxen, and two wagons loaded with enough food for a year. Do you think that will suffice, old boy?"

David added himself and thirty Bakwains to the expedition. And much to the distress of every Boer and every missionary in Africa except himself, once again David was off on a trip to the north. This time he had no less a goal than crossing the Kalahari wilderness to reach the legendary Lake Ngami!

The trip was a familiar one to David as far as the realm of the Bamangwatos. There, Chief Sekomi insisted the white men would die in the Kalahari wilderness. When David persisted, Sekomi insisted on sending two warriors with the expedition.

By June 5, 1849, the caravan passed Serotl, which David considered the gateway to the great Kalahari wilderness, and veered northwest into the wilderness. The next days were tense. The two Bamangwatos moved ahead of the caravan. After a while, David began to suspect they were scaring off native Bushmen who might have guided the caravan to water. Sekomi had not objected to David going north to the Bakaas, but for some reason he didn't want David to encroach upon the Kalahari.

Oswell wasn't perturbed at all. "I'll bet the chief is hiding a great ivory territory!"

They pushed farther and farther. The pace was even slower than usual. The oxen could be driven no more than a few hours after dawn and a few hours before dusk. They were moving a paltry six miles a day. Natives knew of locations where water pooled four or five feet underground on natural "pans" of sand hardened by lime. Holes had to be dug to the limey "pans" to water the stock. A careless shovel would puncture the "pan" and the water would drain right through into the depths. Even with care they were finding only enough water for the horses but not enough for the oxen. Game in the area was the kind that lived far from water: gemsboks, duikers, and springbucks. If only they could see the tracks of zebra, buffalo, or rhino. Those animals were never far from water.

Finally, the travelers were in dire straits. They could not backtrack the oxen to their last water. It was too far. And no water was in sight. They found the juicy striped melons but not nearly enough of them to satisfy their huge contingent of men and animals. Not only did it seem the expedition would fail, there was increasing doubt they would get back at all.

Then both David and Cotton Oswell spotted a figure running through the brush in the distance. "Lion?" asked Oswell.

"It's human. It must be a Bushman!" cried David, who could now distinguish one life form from another, not by actually seeing them but by the way they moved.

Oswell spurred his horse after the fleeing form. His horse easily ran down the fugitive. He escorted the small figure back. "It's a woman of the Bushmen," yelled Oswell.

David calmed her fears by giving her meat and beads. *Where is water?* he gestured. Of course she knew where water was located. Every Bushman knew where to find water. She led them eight miles to a spring. And better than that, not far beyond the spring stretched a gleaming ribbon across the wilderness.

"Is it another mirage?" asked Oswell. They had been fooled before.

"This mirage seems forested along its banks," answered David hopefully. "I'll ask our Bushman." But when he looked around for the woman she was gone.

The next day they inched toward the gleaming ribbon with its green borders. The horses and oxen became very agitated. The oxen sped up. It could only mean one thing. "The animals smell water!" cried David.

The caravan soon reached a village of natives called Bakuratsi on the Zouga River. The river was thirty yards wide and no more than chest deep. But it was precious treasure of clear cold water in the wilderness. And trees towered on its banks. David measured the circumference of one giant tree at seventy feet! Africa was such a wonder. One day a traveler despaired in arid wilderness, the next day he rejoiced in Eden. . . .

David managed to find out that many miles upstream was a lake so large a Bakuratsi once traveled along its banks all day and it still stretched to the western horizon. This very same Zouga River flowed *out of* the lake! A river that flowed *out of* a lake? Could the natives be trusted? Had the two Bamangwatos been here first to spread lies?

David and the others felt there was little to risk now. Maybe they were being tricked into heading the wrong direction but water was plentiful. Supplies of food they had in plenty. Fruit, game, and fish seemed in abundance all along the river. A few days later, Oswell shot a monstrous bull elephant with tusks to match. "Biggest tusker I ever saw," said Oswell, who had hunted many years. "One tusk weighs 107 pounds; the other weighs only a pound less."

They left one wagon behind and pushed west. The natives along the river lived their lives in huts and canoes. They spoke a language that had almost no words in common with the Sechuana dialect of Bantu. Yet when David saw a major river empty into the Zouga from the north, he managed to figure out that the lands the local natives claimed were lush forests and great wide rivers. That astonished him! Great rivers in the center of Africa? Perhaps river commerce could open up Africa and spread the gospel. It so overwhelmed him that when they found Lake Ngami, a vast lake seventy miles long but only chest deep, he was only mildly interested.

He confided in Oswell, "This lake could not be navigated by ships of any size."

"Ship! Did you say ship?" exclaimed Oswell, as if he couldn't believe his ears.

Upon his return to Kolobeng, David sent the London Missionary Society a detailed manuscript of his journey, apprehensive, even defensive, because he had never asked permission of anyone for such a venture. But he had to tell the Society about the great rivers in central Africa. The more he thought about their potential, the more obsessed he became. Yes, they might very well be the conduits of the gospel for Africa. And he didn't doubt for a moment that great rivers abounding with fish and game had to have huge populations of Africans.

That summer Moffat brought to Kolobeng the Reverend John Freeman, one of the London Directors of the London Missionary Society. The utter disappointment in Freeman's eyes stung David's heart. He remembered his own amazement that Moffat had only forty converts in twenty years. Now here was David at Kolobeng, after eight years of contact with the Bakwains, with *one* true convert, a few pretenders, and thousands of unrepentant heathens.

Disillusioned with his accomplishments at Kolobeng, David went north again in 1850. He had many things yet to do. He wanted to go beyond the Zouga River to find Sebitoane, the great chief of the Makalolos. Oswell missed David's departure and found him only on his return. David's second trip north took even Cotton Oswell's breath away.

"Are you sure it was wise to take your family, old boy?" asked Oswell.

"They're Africans. And you should have heard the criticism from the other missionaries when I left them behind on the first trip."

"But until a couple of years ago no whites had ever succeeded in making this journey at all."

"God provides."

Enduring the second trip with David and Mary had been four-year-old Robert, three-year-old Agnes, and Thomas, a babe in arms. The second trip accomplished little more than the first. David still was not able to find Sebitoane. Back at Kolobeng, Mary gave birth to daughter Elizabeth within one month. The infant died a month later.

"The trip north had nothing to do with our sweet little blue-eyed Elizabeth's death," insisted David to Robert Moffat at Kuruman, where he took Mary to convalesce. "The sweet little thing died from a respiratory sickness rampant among the Bakwains at Kolobeng. In fact, the poor little dear would have had a better chance of surviving had we still been in the wilderness."

"What do you plan to do next?" asked Moffat, obviously

confused by David's logic.

"I am planning another trip north to the Zouga River this next winter season. I must find Sebitoane."

David could tell Robert Moffat was biting his tongue. Surely, Moffat hoped, David would not take Mary and the children again. "I suppose you know best, Livingstone. We can't all stay in one place and try to convert the natives. Of course, I don't mean that as a criticism. Have you received word from the Royal Geographic Society in London?"

"No. Has something happened?"

"Yes, Livingstone. They've awarded you their annual Gold Medal for finding Lake Ngami. You also have a medal from a society in Paris. The London Missionary Society is ecstatic with you, Livingstone. Apparently your exploits have caused donations to pour in." But David's frowning father-in-law did not sound like a man offering praise.

David was not anxious to talk about personal awards. Taking Mary and the children had earned him the scorn of every missionary in Africa. When it became known Mary had been pregnant, few remained silent. When it became known the baby had died and Mary had suffered some kind of stroke after the baby was born, their protests were vehement. They were fully prepared for David's next trip north, but they were unprepared for David's fellow travelers.

Even Cotton Oswell was disturbed. "Are you sure you want to take your family again, old boy?"

"Of course. Do you think they will be safer here at Kolobeng? There are sicknesses here, too. And the Boers are a bigger threat to Mary here than the natives on the trail. Besides, Sechele has been talking of moving his village. The soil is not good for corn at Kolobeng. What would Mary do if the whole village of Bakwains pulled out?"

"But couldn't you have Mary and the children stay at Kuruman?"

"My wife does not wish that. She has left the nest. Besides, if there is a problem, she will be with the only medical doctor north of Cape Town and Port Elizabeth. Me. You'll see, Oswell. Everything will go swimmingly."

Mrs. Moffat had written him a blunt angry letter. She knew Mary was pregnant once again. But nothing hurt David more than Oswell's mild disapproval. Oswell himself was fearless, having narrowly escaped death a dozen times. On a previous trip, the massive foot of a charging elephant had missed his head by inches as he was sprawled in the grass. Another time, a rhino's horn had impaled a horse right from under Oswell. He was intelligent, mild-mannered, yet fully as fearless as David himself. And it was only in the most casual way that Oswell even mentioned his brushes with death. David valued his friendship very much.

They left Kolobeng on April 24, 1851. Oswell rode ahead to dig out the "pans" to water the stock. When David and the rest of the caravan caught up with him at a pan, Oswell had little to say until they sat around the evening campfire.

"Had a bit of an interesting experience yesterday," Oswell said matter-of-factly.

"Oh?" commented David, recognizing that Oswell must have quite a hair-raising story to tell.

NINE

"Lions, old boy." Oswell sipped his tea. "Before yesterday, for several nights running while I was camped on this pan, several lions seemed intent on eating my horse. The beasts lurked in the moonless void, roaring like banshees night after night. That makes it a bit difficult to sleep. Yesterday morning, I went after them."

Five-year-old Robert's eyes grew large. "On your horse?"

"Yes, Robert, my lad," answered Oswell. "I took my dogs of course. The good old hounds brought one of the lions to bay in some thick thorn scrub." He laughed. "That lion bolted and found me before I found it. My horse wheeled and I caught my sleeve on a thorn bush. Yanked me right out of the saddle. Knocked me cuckoo. . ."

"What happened?" cried Robert.

"When I woke up, the lion was just thirty yards away, raging like a demon. The dogs had it surrounded again. Good old hounds."

"What happened to the lion?" asked Robert.

"Oh, I was still groggy and I missed the shot. It got away. Hounds made a good show of it, even if I didn't."

On May 8th, the caravan reached the scheming Sekomi and his Bamangwatos. But this time Sekomi had an infected sore on his stomach and he was not about to offend David, the white shaman. So David doctored him. On his way out of the village, David estimated 932 huts and recorded that fact in his notes. He had made up his mind to take better notes, motivated by the enthusiasm for his trip to Lake Ngami. A few people actually seemed interested in what he was doing. So he began to record his exact longitude and latitude every few nights. He always recorded data on water pans, springs, rivers, and wildlife.

One night, they camped by a spring that fed water to a surface pool. Upon hearing the constant chirp of frogs David told the children, "That is the sweetest symphony in all of Africa. It means water, precious water."

Stretches without water, a stomach-churning worry on previous trips, no longer bothered David. He and Oswell now knew where the pans were located, and Oswell continued to ride ahead on horseback to dig them out. For the third time, they entered the village of the Bakuratsi on the Zouga.

Mary sighed. "David, hasn't this chief refused to let you cross the river each time you've been here?"

"Yes, I remember that, too," agreed Robert.

David smiled. "And do you remember the story of the wicked judge in the eighteenth chapter of Luke?"

From memory Mary said, "And there was a widow in that city; and she came unto him, saying, Avenge me of mine adversary. And he would not for a while: but afterward he said within himself, Though I fear not God, nor regard man; Yet because this widow troubleth me, I will avenge her, lest by her continual coming she weary me."

David added, "Pray to God, children, that this is our time for justice."

And this time the chief let David cross.

"It was like a miracle," said Mary.

"Disguised in the drab wrappings of man," commented David. "Apparently the chief of the Bakuratsi knows a group of traders are also looking for Sebitoane. This chief of the Bakuratsi fears Sebitoane very much. He is afraid the traders will sell Sebitoane many rifles for ivory. So he wants us to get up there, too, and convert Sebitoane into a man of peace as quickly as possible. Which is exactly what I intend to do."

Perseverance was one of David's greatest gifts. He never gave up easily. He was not inflexible. He had proved that he was flexible by moving his mission twice. But usually he patiently tried again and again. Always polite, as a man of God should be.

They crossed an enormous salt pan called Ntwetwe. The new guide they had enlisted at the Zouga said it was at least three days in crossing. Their heavy wagons broke through the crust again and again and they toiled in the dry heat to free them. But the caravan continued—always onward. It was early June, and the nights were frosty. But when they left the great pan, they entered a sea of grass with islands of brush. Zebras and wildebeest were abundant.

On June 7th, they entered Goosimjarrah, a village of Bushmen. The Bushmen appeared well fed. Of all natives David encountered, Bushmen were always the merriest. They seemed constantly joshing each other and laughing. And he had never known a Bushman to lie. If only missionaries could master Nama, their very difficult language of clicks.

The Livingstone children got an extra day to enjoy the village. The next day was Sunday.

"We never travel on Sunday," said four-year-old Agnes, already a veteran of the trail.

On Monday, they left with Shobe, a guide from the village. Shobe was the most unusual guide David ever had. If Shobe felt like sleeping during the day, he would simply lie down under a bush and go to sleep. One day the caravan weaved erratically back and forth. David discovered Shobe was following elephant tracks! One day Shobe disappeared. The next day, he reappeared. Finally, the caravan seemed surrounded by endless thorny scrub in all directions. David began to doubt Shobe—not his honesty but his understanding of where David wanted to go. David had his caravan begin to travel at night, keying on stars of the Northern Bear.

"Thank God, I've found rhino tracks," said Oswell one morning, grinning from ear to ear. He always rode ahead. "We are near water."

Brushy grassland yielded to marsh. Soon they found the Mababe River, which flowed north. Natives along the river were not Bushmen, but Kalakas of Chief Chombo. They lived in two-storied huts. At times, the mosquitoes were so bad these Kalakas lit a fire on the first floor and slept in the smoky upper floor. But when frost was on the ground, as it was now, the mosquitoes were dormant.

That was not true of the tsetse fly. The caravan had reached the realm of the notorious insect. Chombo told them it was safe to travel through infestations of the tsetse at night. They rested another Sunday with the villagers and continued on, traveling at night. During the day they rested, with someone always watching their stock for the beelike tsetse flies.

Finally, the travelers saw the wide Chobe River. They were expected by the Makalolos, who spoke a dialect of Bantu. Several of Sebitoane's subchiefs escorted them down the

Chobe in canoes. The river was so wide and deep it harbored hippos as well as crocodiles. The canoes stopped at an island that belonged to Maunko, one of Sebitoane's wives. Natives were sing-ing. The song was very pleasant, not jarring like the sharp yiping of vowels in the songs of the southern tribes. And yet, the Makalolos were much more savage in their appearance and demeanor.

There stood the great chief himself. He was a tall, wiry man of about forty-five.

"We come in peace," said David in Sechuana and extended his hand.

This gesture caught Sebitoane completely by surprise. But after the slightest pause, he was quick-witted enough to grasp David's hand. He was smiling but demanded bluntly, "Tell me why you are here."

In Sechuana David told the chief his objectives: to bring the message of the gospel, to encourage Sebitoane not to deal in slaves, and to encourage the end of wars.

The chief smiled but his words were harsh. "I thought you were here to teach me how to use guns. That is how we Makalolos will make peace."

David explained, "We do not sell guns."

"You are not what I expected. We have much to tell each other." And as they ate porridge and beef, Sebitoane began telling his visitors the story of his life. It was not brief. He talked into the night, allowing David to take notes. Many years before he was only a minor subchief. In 1823, he actually took part in an attack on Kuruman. Robert Moffat was there! The Griquas came with rifles and drove Sebitoane and his natives back to the north. Over the years, he fought the Zulus, the Bamangwatos, the Bakhatlas, the Bakuratsi, and every other tribe. He lost some battles and won others. Sebitoane eventually worked his way north, settling into the area round the Sesheke River. This Chobe River, so wide and deep, was a mere tributary to the mighty Sesheke. Along the Sesheke lived Sebitoane's Makalolos on islands and in marshes. Even the Zulus could not defeat them in their realm. Just the previous year Sebitoane himself had fought Zulus hand to hand on the Sesheke River. His people prospered in spite of river fever.

"It is the strongest tribe in southern Africa," said Oswell agreeably.

David learned Sebitoane was friendly with all visitors—at first. But with the slightest treachery, a visitor was dead. His stories revealed that he was extraordinarily shrewd. He might have lost a battle or two when he was younger, but he was never outwitted. Now he never lost battles.

After Sebitoane finished talking the next morning, he wished to see their caravan to see if it could be ferried to the north side of the Chobe. The south bank was vulnerable to attacks from Zulus. So they canoed back up the Chobe, David clutching his precious detailed history of one of the greatest chiefs of Africa.

When Sebitoane saw their wagons he said, "We cannot ferry such large things." Then he examined their oxen. "They have all been bitten by the tsetse fly. That's too bad."

"But we watched them so carefully during the day," protested David, "and we traveled only at night."

"Someone lied to you. Tsetses bite at night." Sebitoane pointed. "See the swelling over the eyes?" He felt under the jaws of each ox. "This too is swollen. Soon water will run from their eyes and mouth."

David's joy in finding a great chief with such wisdom was cut short. Sebitoane himself became ill. He smoked hashish and coughed, but now he had a fever, too.

"I suffered the same sickness last winter," he told David nonchalantly.

"Don't you have some medicine for Sebitoane?" Oswell asked David later in private.

"I don't dare start doctoring him now. I think he has chronic bronchitis from smoking that devilish hashish year after year. Do you see how emaciated he is? His fever may be the onset of pneumonia, which I can't cure. I have no choice but to let his own shamans doctor him."

"I understand perfectly, old boy. If he were to die under your care, we would all be killed."

"Precisely, Oswell."

And when Sebitoane began to cough green phlegm, David knew the great chief not only had pneumonia but was likely to die. Sebitoane's three shamans cut his skin in fifty places to bleed him. They thought that treatment was what cured him the year before.

On July 7th, a Sunday, David visited Sebitoane, who was lying inside a hut almost too weak to lift his arm in greeting. The chief saw little Robert and said, "Take Robert to Maunko's house and get some milk for him."

Later that day Sebitoane died.

David mourned the great chief. Another soul lost! It was heartbreaking. If only he could have met Sebitoane sooner. The chief had great intellect like Sechele. Surely he would have accepted the truth of the gospel. Surely he would have given up the terrible hashish. Saint Paul's warning in Second Corinthians would have been sufficient to a believer: "Dear friends, let us purify ourselves from everything that contaminates body and spirit, perfecting holiness out of reverence for God."

Now it was too late. It was this sense of tragic urgency that hung over David's head all the time. Africans were dying everywhere, souls lost to eternity. What could be more heart-breaking than that? Yet other white men wondered why he took such chances. If only they saw the tragedy the way he saw it!

And why did Sebitoane have to die? For thirty years, Sebitoane dodged death almost daily. For many years David had wanted to seek him. And for several years David did seek him. Now, after finding him, death claimed him in just sixteen days! What did it mean?

David was yanked from his remorse a week later. He came upon an elephant. Of all the animals in Africa, the elephant was the most unnerving. Its charge could not be stopped without a fusillade of bullets. One or two bullets never dropped an elephant. And all the while it charged, its hellish bellow froze the very soul of its victim. The bellow screamed like a thousand sirens. Horses froze in their tracks. Men's fingers froze on triggers. A charging elephant was like a preview of the wrath of God.

This elephant veered away from David.

"We seem immortal till our work is done," commented David to Oswell later in a thin voice.

David and the caravan stayed on with the Makalolos. Every day, David took notes. His oxen began dying just as Sebitoane had predicted. And David saw sights that would haunt him forever: slaves in chains. He soon learned the exchange rate. One boy was worth about nine yards of good cotton cloth from the slave traders. But a musket was so precious it might cost as much as ten boys.

"Oswell," said David. "To think that cotton cloth I once manufactured is used for such a purpose. If only honest traders could get to the interior of Africa this slave traffic would stop." David could not get that idea out of his mind. It seemed Africa had to be opened to traders with goods that the natives craved. Trade was the key to spreading the gospel and stopping war and slavery. But few traders would travel the harsh way David traveled. How would trade ever reach Africa?

A jaunt to the east with Oswell and their Makalolo companions brought the answer home forcefully. There they saw the Sesheke River. Right there in the center of Africa was a colossal river five hundred yards wide!

"Praise God, Oswell. Do you suppose this Sesheke is the upper reaches of the Zambesi?"

"The great river that flows into the Indian Ocean at Mozambique, old boy? Yes, It's very possible."

"Probable," added David as he thought about it more.

The answer to all of Africa's problems hit David like a bull elephant: This great river—if it flowed all the way into the Indian Ocean—would bring traders. And why wouldn't it reach all the way east? It was a mighty river here among the Makalolos, and it would only get larger as it picked up more tributaries.

In August, five weeks after Sebitoane died, the caravan headed south again. The days would get hotter and finally by November, the summer rain would begin. They could not delay any longer. Knowing where water was located and knowing which areas to avoid made a great difference in crossing wilderness. In just two weeks, they reached the Zouga River.

On September 15, still along the banks of the Zouga, Mary gave birth to a boy. They named him William Oswell after their good friend, but David nicknamed the boy "Zouga."

A few days later, Thomas got "river fever." The temperatures along the river during that day were above 100 degrees. David moved the caravan to hills above the river where it was cooler. He wrapped Thomas in damp sheets and made sure he drank plenty of water. Then he gave him doses of quinine. They stayed there nearly a month. Finally, Thomas and the baby Zouga were both healthy enough to travel.

When they reached Kolobeng, David's fears about Sechele moving his village were justified. Sechele had moved twelve miles from Kolobeng. David's mission at Kolobeng was now isolated. All the way back from Sebituane's country, David had thought about finding rivers to open the interior of Africa. His lack of converts after ten years made his decision to continue exploring the north country easy. But there was the very grave decision as to where Mary and the children should live. Isolated Kolobeng was no longer an option. Bringing the children on further trips was not an option, either. Next time, he might not get back south again for a very long time.

David broke the news to Mary. "Mary, you must take the children and go live with my parents in Scotland."

"Scotland!"

"Yes. Unless you wish to stay at Kuruman."

"I can't live as both a mother and a child. I'll go to Scotland."

David was glad Mary so readily agreed. The children would now get a real education. No Livingstone he ever knew, no matter how poor, ever neglected the education of his children. Even his grandfather, poor as any wretch could be fresh off a failed farm in Ulva, found the pennies to educate seven children. And his father, Neil, had done the very same thing. No Livingstone child—boy or girl—would face life without the power of literacy.

He didn't have to explain to Mary he would rarely be at Kolobeng any more, either. Mary knew exactly what he had in mind. She told him, "I know you intend to explore central

Africa. And I approve. But it is still very difficult. Yet, I am a missionary's daughter. I know a great deal about separations."

Mary didn't have to reveal all her thoughts to David. By now he knew what she was thinking. She had lived six active years with him; she had four healthy children. She and David would resume their life after he explored awhile. And like every young married woman of her day, she knew together-ness meant constant pregnancies followed by ever increasing toil. Being separated had its blessings, too. David knew she was thinking of that, as well.

They stayed in Kuruman for three weeks. Mary's brother Robert was there now, newly married. In January of 1852, the Livingstones went southwest. Traveling that civilized route by ox wagon was always pleasant, like a succession of picnics. They reached Cape Town March 16th. But David could not get his family on a ship that sailed any sooner than the middle of April.

He was not one to be idle. His throat was so bad now he could not speak in public. So he had his uvula removed. Then to make sure information gathered on his trip was not in vain, he wrote a paper about the "region north of Lake Ngami" and sent it to the Royal Geographic Society. He was sorely tempted to call the Sesheke River the Zambesi River but resisted. Cape Town astronomer Thomas Maclear taught him how to make very sophisticated measurements of latitude and longitude in the field with a chronometer and sextant.

He even had his first photographs taken. Studying two proofs he said, "Unfortunately, the ugliest of the two is most like the original." And he marveled at his own smug look in the photographs.

He soon discovered it was a good thing he could not speak in public. He was well known enough to be hated by whites in Cape Town, especially Dutch Boers. He was known as the trouble-making missionary who opposed slavery and treated black Africans like equals. He was said to be an exceedingly dangerous man, poking about in the wilds, probably wanting to sell guns to the heathen next. The entire London Missionary Society was hated. But David was by far the most aggressive, by far the most dangerous, and by far the worst.

The atmosphere of hatred made watching his family sail away from Cape Town easier. As much as he was now hated by the Boers and many others, too, how safe were Mary and the children on the frontier of South Africa? And did he want them to grow up in an area where their father was hated by whites?

"Praise the Lord and friend Oswell, they won't go back to Scotland looking like shabby paupers," muttered David as he watched the ship sail. Through the generosity of steadfast Oswell, Mary and the children had embarked in brand new wardrobes.

David had many delays while at Cape Town, often due to deliberate mischief by Boers. That and the prevailing hatred made him sour and anxious to get back to Kolobeng. He didn't reach Kuruman until September. It had been one year since Zouga's birth. He felt he had accomplished almost nothing in one whole year toward opening Africa to the gospel.

But at Kuruman a letter Robert Moffat had received changed his mind completely. . . .

TEN

The letter from Sechele read:

My friend of my heart's love. . .I am undone by the Boers, who have attacked me, though I have no guilt with them. They required that I should be in their kingdom but I refused. They demanded that I should prevent the English and southern tribes from passing through to the north. . . . They began on Monday morning at twilight and fired with all their might and burned the village with fire and scattered us. They killed 60 of my people and captured women and children and men. . .and they took all the cattle and all the goods of the Bakwains. . .the house of Livingstone, they also plundered, taking all his goods. . . .

How little David had suffered compared to faithful Sechele. But if David had not been delayed at Cape Town and had been at Kolobeng, isolated as it now was from Sechele's warriors, he surely would have been killed. Was that why God delayed him at Cape Town? Yes, he was sure of it. Another brush with death. Yet spared by Providence. How evil the Boers were!

He couldn't even return to Kolobeng to visit his daughter Elizabeth's grave. Boers were still in the vicinity. They had gone to Kolobeng first. With four wagons they methodically stole all David's furniture, medical supplies, tools, and food. Then they maliciously ripped apart all his journals and papers and burned them. Then the Boers went after Sechele and his Bakwains.

"These stories about the Boers aren't making it easy to find natives to accompany me back to Sebitoane's country," David complained to Robert Moffat. "The Boers want to cut us off from the north, but they will not succeed."

Moffat was subdued. "Our own government has given up on doing anything with the wilderness. The Boers know that."

Over the days, David collected a retinue of natives. His main companion was a West Indies mulatto named George Fleming. Fleming was a solid man, but the six natives seemed a poor lot. Who else would venture into the teeth of the Boers?

One night in Kuruman, David poured his anguish into his journal:

> *Am I on my way to die in Sebitoane's country? Have I seen the end of my wife and children?—the breaking up of all connections to earth, leaving this fair and beautiful world, and knowing so little of it? I am only learning the alphabet of it yet, and entering on an untried state of existence. Following Him who entered before me into the*

clouds, the veil, is a serious prospect. Do we begin again in our new existence to learn much from experience, or have we full powers? My soul, where will you migrate? Where will you lodge the first night after leaving this body? Will an angel soothe your flutterings? for sadly flurried will you be in entering eternity. . . Oh Jesus, fill me with Your love now, and I beseech You accept me, and use me a little for Your glory. I have done nothing for You yet, and I would like to do something. . . .

In December, he left Kuruman with two ox-wagons. Leaving in the height of summer betrayed his overpowering desire to push north. He skirted Kolobeng and farther on stayed with the Bakwains for two weeks. He was delighted to see Bakwains were reading the Bible. Good Sechele. But Sechele was not there. Encouraged by Moffat, Sechele had gone to Cape Town to demand justice. David, who had just been in Cape Town, knew scant justice waited for a black African in Cape Town.

One morning in the Kalahari wilderness, David awoke to discover all his oxen had disappeared. Kibopecoe, one of the Bakwain men, was gone, too. It was March 19, 1853, David's 40th birthday. The next morning, Kibopecoe returned, driving all the oxen. A huge hyena had stampeded the oxen into the wilderness. Kibopecoe had been on his feet for thirty-six hours. Praise God, thought David, for such a stout-hearted man. He had judged the six helpers too soon.

The trip through the Kalahari was severe in the heat of summer. In the first weeks he shot steinbucks, impalas, an eland, and even giraffes to feed his men. Some of these animals came to the pans they had dug out to water the oxen. The poor animals were willing to risk death for the water they smelled. David never killed an animal without regretting it.

And these particular animals, so desperate to drink, hurt most of all.

David loved the creatures of nature. They revealed God's miraculous creativity. At one spot north of the Zouga River, he was enthralled by a nest he found. The bird had taken green leaves and woven them together with threads from a spider's web. The bird actually punctured the leaves with its beak, inserted thread through the holes and somehow thickened the ends into knots! God's unseen hand was everywhere.

By May of 1853, he saw a wonderful sight. "It's the Chobe River!" he called to George Fleming.

Over six thousand natives welcomed him in the main village of Linyanti. The Makalolos had planted a special garden for him, which was now choked with corn. Women immediately began shelling it and grinding cornmeal for him. Yet the atmosphere was thick with worry, too. The new chief of the Makalolos was Sebitoane's son Sekeletu, a youth of eighteen. Sekeletu had inherited a title to a realm he might never merit. It was rumored some warriors were plotting against him.

In that aura of treachery, David came down with the river fever for the first time. He almost welcomed it. He would see if the Makalolo shamans had some marvelous native remedy. But he soon wrote:

> . . .*after being stewed in their vapor bathes, smoked like a red herring over green twigs, and charmed. . .I concluded that I could cure the fever more quickly than they can. There is a good deal in not "giving in" to this disease. He who is low-spirited, and apt to despond at every attack, will die sooner. . . .*

David resolved that he would act as if he were not sick at

all. He had much to do. By canoe—fever or no fever—he ventured north up the wide Sesheke River into the Barotse Valley to find a location for a mission away from the deadly fever-breeding marshes. He knew that much about the cause of the fever. Its outbreaks were concentrated around stagnant waters of the marshes.

Sekeletu went with him. The intrigue continued. One night Sekeletu confided to David, "My half brother Mpepe intends to kill me." David had met Mpepe before. He was a braggart and so disrespectful that Sebitoane himself had told David, "If he ever treats my son Sekeletu with such disrespect he will be killed." David knew Sebitoane was rarely wrong about anything.

Suddenly, by the side of the fire right in front of David, Sekeletu's warriors seized Mpepe, dragged him to the outskirts of camp, and speared him to death. David was shocked. He had not even had a chance to rise and protest. The execution was so precipitous. Had Sekeletu taken advantage of David's presence? Perhaps David had triggered it. Maybe rivals were saying the white shaman's approval of Sekeletu would strengthen his hold on power, so Sekeletu must be brought down as soon as possible. David convinced himself Mpepe had been conspiring to kill Sekeletu. Still, he would watch the young chief carefully.

The lack of a suitable site for a mission and David's recurring fever tested his resolve. The fever began like a common cold but soon its victim had racking pain in the neck and back, often with a throbbing headache. The pained areas grew hot with fever, yet the victim felt chills. Vomiting was frequent. Ulcers formed around the mouth. Then the victim burned with fever but could not sweat. Finally, profuse sweating broke the fever but left its victim debilitated. About when the poor soul felt healthy, the disease flared up again to run the same painful course. Each morning David greeted the dawn with a reminder from Proverbs 17: "A merry heart doeth good like a medicine." It served him well through seven attacks of river fever in nine weeks!

David was never idle no matter how bad he felt. If he was too weak to leave his tent, he worked on his journal. He synthesized observations of twelve years. Although some Europeans had speculated many species of rhinoceros, David clearly saw two species, each with two varieties. He not only described each variety in detail physically, but he recorded their habits. The *Mohohoo*, or white rhino, avoided fights but the *Boreele*, or black rhino, attacked savagely—even elephants! David's knowledge was not secondhand. His own wagon had been attacked twice by black rhinos. He even knew exactly which plants each species of rhino ate:

> *The chief food [of the white rhino] is grass, but to this they add the tender shoots of some trees. Such are the* Monokane *and* Makabe *(gum yielding), and* Morupaphiri *(a short thorn),* Moguana *(sweet),* Mosilabele *(bitter), and* Morolane *(a solaneum narcotic). The grasses of which he is most fond are called* Mosegashue *and* Tlokwane.

David even described the kinds of worms they carried in their intestines. He described how they ran. Was it a canter? A trot? He recorded what to do if pursued by one. He described how their flesh tasted.

There was no large mammal that he did not describe succinctly. Yet he saw the small creatures, too. He knew if termites were rushing out of their mounds to retrieve straw it meant rain was imminent. He recognized fifteen varieties of ants and termites, noting that they occurred in great abundance. Of his variety III, described as "black with a tint of gray, one-half inch long," he wrote:

> The large black ants go on marauding expeditions against them [termites]. The army is usually about 3 to 6 inches broad and about 6 feet in length. They make a chirping or hissing noise, and from the manner in which they run about when disturbed in their march, seem ready for all the exploits of "brutal soldiery." In a short time they may be seen returning, each with a [termite] in its mandibles. The captive catches hold on all the blades of grass along the route, but the black is the stronger one, and the prisoner can scarcely retard the progress of the victor beyond the space requisite for a vigorous tug. . . . Indeed I saw one army in a cold damp morning which had removed the legs of the [termites] that they might be the more easily carried. And another on a warm day seemed to have stung all their captives and probably injected the same substance as the Mason bee or dauber [wasp] does into the caterpillar which it deposits for the food of its young. . . .

Of course, David recorded even more observations about the Africans. Many of their customs weighed heavily on him. The killing of babies by the Bakaas because they cut their upper teeth before they cut their lower teeth was almost too barbarous to record. There were many heartbreaking realities every day with the Makalolos that made the spread of the gospel urgent:

Having gone into town as usual today, I saw a woman and two boys brought into the kotla *[council] for distribution. When taken the woman must have been stripped of all her clothing, for she had only a piece of a sort of gunney bag on, 2 inches broad. Her child was about one year old. The party from which she was brought. . .were killed and these three brought here. . . . Oh, miserable Africa! How much need there is for the gospel. . . .*

And just days later he wrote:

A poor girl in a state of destitution lay near my path to the town. . . . I told her to go to the wagon and I gave her some food. . . . She came several times and I spoke to her owner about her. He complained of want of food himself, but being a rich man I thought it was only talk. The wretched girl came to the wagon again and again. . . . On asking her owner yesterday where she was, he said she had gone into the field and probably died there of starvation. Poor wretch, this is the fate of many in this benighted land. They wander forth and become the prey of hyenas. . . .

David's frequent sermons were well attended by the Makalolos. He read small passages from the Bible then illustrated what the passages meant with stories. He had a new slide projector that awed the natives even more than his mirror. David called it his "magic lantern." After the sun went down he thrilled the natives with slide shows of scenes from the Bible.

"But the show has become the object of their whole desire," he admitted to himself one evening.

His dissatisfaction with his efforts deepened. Sekeletu not only showed no interest in the gospel, but an aversion. He seemed to already know about the teaching in the Bible that Jesus said a man could have only one wife. Sekeletu had many wives. He enjoyed them very much. When David offered to teach him God's own words out of his Bible in the Sechuana dialect, Sekeletu sent his father-in-law and stepfather in his place.

By November, David was anxious to explore. Once again, he felt he had failed to convert Africans. The painful truth was that they clung fiercely to their native beliefs, protecting their habits of many wives, even the terrible custom of offering a wife to a guest for the night, and worse yet, selling fellow Africans into slavery.

He met slave traders, including the Portuguese Silva Porto. David's stay in Rio de Janeiro had given him enough Portuguese to converse with the aid of much arm waving. Porto was amused when David upbraided him for trading slaves. After all, shrugged Silva Porto, what could one expect a man of the cloth to say? David had more in common with the shrewd Portuguese than he liked to admit. Whereas David was as daring as he was righteous, Porto was as daring as he was evil. He, too, had penetrated where few white men had ever been. He, too, had story after story of rivers and natives—but all to the west, all toward the Portuguese haven of Luanda on the Atlantic Ocean. David had always assumed he would first follow the Sesheke downstream to the Indian Ocean. Now he wanted to try the western passage first.

Sekeletu protested David's plans to leave. "Why depart? I hear there are Makalolos who can give your sermons by heart."

"I'll find a great river. Then I will follow it west. To the

Atlantic Ocean. Perhaps honest traders—not traders in slaves—will come to you on that river to gladden your heart."

"The slave traders have a well-worn route to that great water to the west."

"I can't follow the slave route. The slave traders know I am against slavery. That route is too dangerous for me now. And the people along the route are probably corrupted. I will go west—but I must go north first."

"It is death to go north!"

"I can't use my ox-wagons. I need men and canoes."

"I will honor your wish to go north to your death."

Sekeletu's feeling of doom affected David, too. He wrote a few last letters which Sekeletu promised to send south to Kuruman whenever a traveler was available. To his brother-in-law, David wrote, "I shall open a path into the interior—or perish." Three days before his expedition departed, he wrote his father, whom he considered executor of his final will and testament:

> My blessing on my wife. May God comfort her. If my watch comes back after I am cut off, it belongs to Agnes. If my sextant, it is Robert's. The Paris medal to Thomas. Double-barreled gun to Zouga [Oswell]. Be a father to the fatherless. . .for Jesus' sake.

George Fleming was not going with him. He would stay behind to try to establish an ivory trade for the Makalolos with the south. If David could not find a great river route to open commerce, perhaps the lure of ivory could bring honest traders from the south to the Makalolos. They must give the Makalolos incentive to give up trading slaves.

A feeling of impending doom hung over the twenty-seven

Makalolos Sekeletu supplied David as porters. For firearms, the escort carried three muskets, one pistol, and a rifle. One man stayed near David, carrying his huge double-barrel. Their supplies included ammunition, tea, sugar, and coffee. It was in packing for the journey that David discovered much of his supply of medicine had been stolen and traded—by some of the very men he brought with him from Kuruman. He immediately dismissed them, resisting the strong temptation to have Sekeletu mete out Makalolo "justice."

Large tin canisters protected his best clothing, his "magic lantern," and what little medicine remained. His precious instruments were wrapped in waterproof oilskin. The sextant was a fine one made by Troughton and Sims of Fleet Street in London. His chronometer watch was made by Dent of the Strand for the Royal Geographic Society. His telescope was small but could be steadied by screwing the base onto a tree. He also had a Dolland thermometer and two compasses, one which he carried in his pocket.

For his own comfort he took a small tent, a rug for a mattress, a sheepskin blanket, and another canister with his books. His books were the Sechuana Testaments, his own Bible in English, several books for astronomical calculations, and a lined ledger which he used for his journal. The ledger was revealing. On previous trips his lock-clasped ledgers had about 350 pages. But the lock-clasped ledger for this trip had well over 800 pages.

To show confidence in the expedition, Sekeletu gave him ivory tusks. "Exchange them for European goods," said Sekeletu. "Buy me a horse, too." But his eyes showed he never expected to see David again.

Once more David found himself traveling in the heat of the summer. But he spent too much time waiting anyway. The flotilla of canoes started up the steamy Sesheke River into the Barotse Valley. The first sixty miles were familiar. But soon he was passing out of the influence of the Makalolos into the realm of the Balondas. The expedition left the river for a while to bypass Gonye Falls. Further on at the village of Nariel, he ran into a nasty situation. Sekeletu's uncle Mpololo was there, enslaving Balonda natives.

David agonized to himself, "I can try to stop this. But do I dare challenge Mpololo? Does he respect the white shaman friend of Sekeletu? Or does Mpololo think he is far enough away from the young chief to do anything he pleases?" Then David asked God in prayer. The answer came to him: *I must trust God. God doesn't make mistakes.*

David challenged Mpololo. He called a *picho*, a council. He demanded, "Release your captives, Mpololo!"

ELEVEN

Mpololo and his cohorts meekly surrendered Balonda prisoners. "I trusted God," David reminded himself. "And God doesn't make mistakes." He took the prisoners with him. They were from a village upstream.

The country was lush. Seas of grass were interspersed with thick woodlands, even patches of dense forest. The caravan had a routine now. They would rise each morning at five o'clock. In the weak light of dawn, they dressed and made coffee. Then they loaded the canoes and departed. The cool morning was the best part of the day. The men rowed strongly. Yet the speed of the canoes was governed by the speed of oxen being herded along the shore. Not only did the herders have to cut through brush but the Sheskeke River was crawling with fat crocodiles. The great reptiles could launch their one thousand pounds completely clear of the water to snap razored jaws on an unsuspecting animal.

By noon, the travelers stopped to drink water, eat leftovers, and rest an hour. Then the heat of the afternoon gradually wore them and their stock down to an indifferent plod. In the evening, the men secured the canoes and cut grass to cushion David's rug. His various canisters and special supplies were arranged around his bed. They pitched the tent over all of that. The main fire crackled only a man's length from the tent. The Makalolos prepared all meals, which were the food the natives normally ate. David indulged only in coffee or tea. At night, the two fiercest Makalolos slept flanking the tent. Mashauana, the head boatman, slept in front of the flap of the tent. The oxen were placed near the fire, encircled by lean-tos of the sleeping porters.

"We are now completely beyond the influence of Sekeletu," warned Mashauana.

As they approached a village now, they sent an emissary ahead. David knew it was not wise to surprise a village. They had to wait for a welcome, often several days. The river was full of fish. The nearby grasslands teemed with meat on the hoof. So the travelers ate well while waiting. Fever still attacked David. For twelve years, he had suffered only broken bones. His wounds had often been excruciating but they healed. Now suffering seemed constant, alternating from bouts of fever to spells of weakness and dizziness. His quinine, the one thing that seemed to alleviate river fever, had been stolen.

Two days after Christmas, they stopped near the village of the chief named Masiko. It was here the Balonda prisoners belonged. They released the prisoners and proceeded. The new year of 1854 brought David completely into the domain of the Balondas. The main chief in the area was called Shinte. David's friendship with Sekeletu was of no value here. Shinte did not like the Makalolos. . . .

Balondas were already doing him mischief. David stopped and sent word ahead to their nearest chief, Manenko.

She was the niece of Shinte. She sent an envoy to tell him to wait then, after letting him wait several days, sent another envoy ordering him to come to her village.

"We will bypass her," David told his men, in a rare show of temper.

The next village had another female chief, Nyamoana, who was the sister of Shinte and the mother of Manenko. And soon Manenko herself appeared. She was a tall robust woman of twenty. Her husband was her spokesman, constantly rubbing sand on his chest and arms as he greeted them. Other men were thumping their elbows against their ribs.

Once again the travelers were delayed in a whimsical, half-threatening way. When they ran out of food, the Balondas offered them only tasteless tubers for nourishment. David decided to call their bluff and leave. He prided himself on being able to see inside the hearts of Africans. He rarely misjudged them. Being alive was proof of that.

But as he ordered his Makalolos to pack up and launch the canoes, Manenko unloaded such a tirade of abuse on his men, they stopped working. David shrugged and started to load a canoe himself. His example would surely spur them on. Suddenly, he felt a firm hand on his shoulder. It was Manenko, looking at him with pity in her eyes.

She said, "Now, my little man, just do as the rest have done."

Who could resist such motherly concern? But David sensed he must not challenge Manenko's authority. She had handled the situation perfectly. So the travelers waited. After an interval of several days, Nyamoana presented him with a necklace as if she was atoning for their delays. It had a sea shell that was as highly prized by the Balondas as gold was to an Englishman.

A few days later, they thrashed into thick forest behind

Manenko herself to visit the village of Shinte, the head chief of the Balondas. The country could hardly have been more different from the Kalahari wilderness. Vine-draped trees were so dense, the travelers had to hack their way through. And rain, so precious in the south, seemed to fall in buckets.

Manenko set a fast pace. David was sure she had to prove herself constantly to men in the tribe. David had done that once to disbelieving Bakaas. She succeeded, too. Many of the travelers were exhausted. David was spared the exertion by riding his ox Sinbad. Sinbad had a back as soft as a mattress but a nasty disposition. Every time David attempted to use an umbrella in the downpour Sinbad's great curved horn knocked him flying.

After the travelers arrived at the outskirts of Shinte's village, Manenko awaited her uncle's approval to enter. He kept her waiting in what seemed a whimsical fashion. So David now knew it was the custom of Balondas to behave like that with visitors.

Already in Shinte's village were two half-breeds who spoke Portuguese. They were accompanied by native henchmen, the notorious Mambaris, known throughout the interior for their gaudy European prints. Anywhere a member of this tribe was seen in lands where David had visited, slaves were being bought or captured.

"Look!" said David's head boatman, Mashauana, pointing toward the tents of the Portuguese.

"Slaves," groaned David. In front of the tents were women, chained together in dejection. David approached them. "Where are you from?"

"Lobale," answered one woman fearfully.

"That is the hill country to the west," said Mashauana.

The slave traders maintained military discipline, as if this behavior would intimidate the Balondas. A drummer and a bugler performed at regular intervals. When Shinte finally received David, the Portuguese, too, were seeing him for the first time, and they entered drumming, bugling, and firing their rifles in salute.

The kotla was a square one hundred yards on each side. On one end under banyon trees sat Shinte on a throne covered by leopard skins. He was a man, neither small nor large, in his fifties. He wore a checked jacket over a scarlet kilt of coarse, napped cotton. Around his neck hung many strings of beads. Iron and copper bracelets jangled on his arms. Goose feathers plumed over his pillbox cap of fine beads.

David sat down about forty yards away as the Balondas presented themselves to Shinte. They rubbed ashes over their chests and arms. Suddenly, Shinte's warriors ran toward David, screaming, making faces, and brandishing swords. David knew this display served much the same purpose as the lion's bluff. Would the visitors run or stand? After he sat expressionless through the display, the warriors turned to Shinte, politely bowed, and moved aside.

Nyamoana then gave a speech, spiced with exaggerated gestures, telling Shinte everything she knew about David. She began by complimenting David on returning prisoners taken by Mpololo of the Makalolos. She praised him for preaching that tribes should live in peace. She said he had a book that he claimed was the word of God. But then she presented David's flaws. He had preached first to their enemies, the Makalolos.

"So maybe," she finished, "he is telling lies to the Balondas."

The entire time that Nyamoana spoke, a hundred women in the same red fabric sat behind Chief Shinte, often interrupting with laughter or chanting in unison. David had been in councils among African tribes for twelve years. Never before had he seen women even allowed in a council. But he had never seen women as chiefs before, either. The Balondas gave their women many rights.

Also while Nyamoana spoke, three men drummed and four men played a marimba, an instrument with fifteen wooden keys. The faster they played the more excited the gathering became. And Nyamoana was only the first speaker. She was followed by eight others. It was a large council, with over a thousand people gathered around, of which several hundred were warriors.

At long last, Shinte, who had remained as immobile and expressionless as David throughout the speeches, stood up. But he said nothing. The council was over!

The next morning, David was summoned by Shinte. Shinte said, "During the council yesterday I expected a man who claims he is from God to approach me."

David replied, "When I saw your own warriors keep their distance from you, I thought I should do the same. Have you seen a white man before?"

"Never. Some of the slave traders have brown skin. But your skin is white. And your hair is straight like grass. And I have never seen clothes like yours before."

"I wish you to have one of my oxen," David said.

"Yes. I like that kind of meat very much."

"You could have that kind of meat all the time if you kept oxen yourself. This grassy country is very good for cattle."

"But how would I get cattle?"

"Trade with the Makalolos."

"My enemies?"

"Yes."

Suddenly Manenko appeared. She had been invisible ever since David arrived, making him think perhaps she was not in good standing with her uncle Shinte. But she said sharply to Shinte, "This white man belongs to me. Therefore I want the ox." She had her men slaughter the ox right in front of Shinte and left him only one leg.

Shinte seemed amused by her audacity. The wisdom of David's decision weeks ago to yield to Manenko was borne out. She was a favorite of Chief Shinte. She was very powerful among the Balondas.

When David saw Shinte again later, river fever was racking him. The hot rainy weather seemed to aggravate the fever. Shinte said, "I can send men to guide you toward the great water to the west. But if you have the river fever, you won't make it."

"What do you Balondas do for this fever?"

"Drink lots of beer." Shinte offered him a beer they made from corn.

David politely sipped some beer but he did not believe it was a remedy. It only made a man so drunk he forgot the fever for a while. Shinte, now eating beef, spoke again. "This is very good. I will get cattle from Sekeletu. He is like a son to me. I knew Sebitoane very well."

David was surprised to hear Shinte speak favorably of Sebitoane. And his son Sekeletu. Was the belligerence the Balondas expressed toward the Makalolos mere talk and posturing? Or was Shinte not telling the truth? Some chiefs were as deceptive as any white man.

Later, David showed Shinte and his court his slide show. The first image, that of Abraham holding the knife over Isaac, was life-sized. The women of the court began screaming and fled. They thought they, too, would be knifed. They could not be persuaded to return.

Shinte was pleased with the images. "Those look much more like gods than our own gods of clay and wood."

David let Shinte examine the slide projector, so he would know it was only a machine. He did not like to deal in "magic." Shinte also came into his tent in the middle of the night. There he examined David's instruments, the mirror, and every thing he considered exotic. To show his gratitude Shinte gave David a very rare sea shell. "Two of these shells can buy a slave," he bragged.

Later he presented a ten-year-old girl to David. "I have noticed you do not a have child to attend you. Take this girl as my gift."

"I can not take this girl," protested David. Shinte spoke softly to one of his attendants. A few minutes later an older girl was brought to David. "No," said David. "I can not take any child from her parents." He went on to tell Shinte that slavery was bad. People should not be bought and sold. But his message was not reaching Shinte. David always tried to speak bluntly but he did not nag. It was better to remain friends with the chiefs and try to win them over slowly.

After being with Shinte for ten days, he left with Shinte's guide, Intemese. The new guide was not honest, often delaying them for false reasons. But he was useful anyway. Without Intemese to smooth things over, villagers went wild with worry as they saw the caravan approach, more frightened by the Makalolos than David.

The reddish soil was rich in organic matter. The Balondas raised manioc in ridges. It required little care. When they harvested the roots, which were several times larger than a carrot, they started a new plant by simply breaking off a fragment of the stalk and planting it in the freshly created hole. Among the manioc plants, the Balondas planted beans. They paid a price for the ease of manioc. It was incredibly bland, so much so that David had thought it an insult when first given to him by Manenko.

Soon the caravan crossed the Leeba River to enter a vast plain of shallow water with occasional small islands. The travelers needed Intemese more than ever. There seemed no landmarks to go by. At night, when they slept on one of the small islands, they had to build mounds for their beds and ridges around their sleeping areas. If they did not make those tedious preparations they spent a wet night.

They left the saturated plain to reach the realm of the Balonda chief Katema. David already knew the Balondas had recently lost their greatest chief, Matiamvo, much like the Makalolos lost Sebitoane. His death made traveling more dangerous, because the lesser chiefs were suspicious of any new development. Some Balonda chief would try to take the throne, and use of outsiders was always suspected. And Makalolos were regarded as the fiercest kind of savage.

Although the Bolandas spoke a dialect of Bantu, David still had to speak through an interpreter to explain the gospel. Only the slide show had held the interest of Shinte's Bolandas. But Katema would not even permit the slide show. From the outset, Katema seemed very different from Shinte. Further proof was in the fields. He had a herd of splendid white brahma cattle. But he had not domesticated them. They were hunted down like wild game. David explained that they could be tamed, even milked.

"I wish to go on to the great waters to the west," said David finally.

"The plains of Lobale are flooded now. You will have to go north where traders have never gone before. I will give you a guide, Shakatwala."

David preferred to be off the slave route anyway. To show his gratitude to Katema, David had an ox butchered. But

Katema would not eat with him. He would accept the meat to be cooked later by his own people, but he would not eat anything prepared by visitors.

The travelers descended into a watery plain again. Africa was so flat that there were few barriers to travel other than hostile animals or natives. David was used to seeing footpaths everywhere. But on these watery plains the paths disappeared or were in water too deep to follow. So they thrashed through tall grass, which was not only tiring but painful.

When they left the watery plain, David recognized a startling change. Rivers now ran north or west instead of south or east. Cool breezes blew from the north. In all his years in Africa, he had never felt a cool breeze from the north. And the topography changed. He saw the first deep canyon since Kolobeng. By traveling west across north-flowing rivers, the travelers wearily passed in and out of valley after valley.

The natives were different, too. The travelers had entered the realm of Katende. Contrary to Katema's belief that traders never came this way, traders had been here. Katende's people were the most corrupt natives David had seen yet. They would not offer food but only sell it. They knew nothing of money, not even gold. But food was not cheap. For payment they wanted gunpowder or cotton cloth or slaves or tusks or beads or copper rings or sea shells.

One of David's men fell prey to a trick. He found a knife lying on the ground that had been deliberately placed there. Then he was accused of theft. Only one of David's prized sea shells could ransom him.

They continued on their travels, encountering one demand for payment after another. Soon David's Makalolos were giving their own possessions, even their clothing, out of fear of being stranded in such a hostile place. If the caravan ever reached the west coast they might not be wearing anything!

They entered the realm of the Chiboque tribe, still cross-ing north-flowing rivers. David had an ox slaughtered near the village of a chief named Njambi. The meat was for David's own men, who seemed more and more despondent. But David sent the hump and ribs to the chief with the message that it was payment for passing through.

The next day a messenger came from the village to say, "Njambi will not let you pass for anything less than one man, or one ox, or one gun, or plenty of gunpowder, or a sea shell."

David was not amused at such extortion. "I already gave you beef. You get nothing," he said.

By afternoon their camp was surrounded by Chiboque warriors from the village. David saw the chief Njambi coming, with his counselors. David sat down in a camp chair with the huge double-barrel across his lap. Njambi and his contingent sat down across from David. The chief made his demands. David would not have anyone killed over one cotton shirt if that payment would suffice.

"I'll pay you one cotton shirt," he said, gesturing to his own shirt.

Immediately the younger Chiboque warriors protested. They wanted to fight. They were sure they would win. Then they would have everything the travelers owned. So David was persuaded by his own men to add a string of beads to the offer. The Chiboque warriors were outraged. They wanted more. Some were dancing up close, brandishing weapons. Snarls revealed their teeth were filed to points.

"Enough of this!" barked David. He stood and leveled his rifle at Njambi. . . .

TWELVE

Njambi's eyes grew wide. They betrayed he knew those gaping barrels held bullets that could stun an elephant. He had expected none of this. He suddenly was very vulnerable. The Makalolos were near enough to kill him instantly, even if the white man missed.

Njambi began to squirm. He said, "For one ox, we will let you pass."

David could see the chief was telling the truth. David was very angry, but he would let no man die for one ox. So he agreed. After they left the Chiboques, David stopped in the hills to talk with his Makalolos.

He said, "We must continue west without the aid of villagers. Soon we will have nothing left."

"And then you will have to give them one of us," complained one of the Makalolos.

"We will never give up men," insisted David. "We won't fight to save an ox, but we will fight to save a man."

So they continued on to the west. David suffered from

river fever again. And ornery Sinbad took advantage of his weakness, often ducking under a low branch to scrape him off, then trying to kick him. The only thing that kept Sinbad from being the first ox butchered long ago was the fact that his back was spongy soft.

David was in the clutches of burning fever now. Finally he was unable to travel. They camped. Once on awakening he overheard mutiny among his men. Some said it was time to go back, before it was too late.

David rushed out, brandishing a pistol. "There will be no more talk like that," he growled, trying not to show how dizzy he was.

He forced himself to travel further. It was when they were camped, making no progress at all, that the men lost heart. But again he collapsed. They camped on the banks of the Loajima River. David fell into fitful sleep. He awoke to total silence.

"The men have abandoned me," he moaned. "God help me now." He stumbled out of his tent. "You *are* here," he exclaimed in gratitude. His men had built a stockade. "What is happening?" asked David.

Mashauana answered, "We are surrounded by Chiboques."

They could have abandoned me, he thought to himself. *Yet they stayed. Praise the Lord for that.*

David parleyed with the Chiboques. Once again, they wanted a man, an ox, a tusk, or a gun. David offered copper rings. The Chiboques would settle for nothing less than an ox.

"I should give them Sinbad," said David, remembering the cantankerous animal. "Tell them I agree. But don't give them Sinbad."

Once again, they pushed on. David was so sick now he no longer cared if he was attacked or not. But he knew he could not collapse in his tent and wait for the fever to break. It wasn't fair to his men. He had to get them out of the country of the Chiboques. Once more Sinbad scraped David off his back, but this time his kick battered David's thigh. And constant wetness had chaffed David's skin to a bloody abrasion. He was nearly an invalid, but he forced himself to continue on.

And then they found themselves stopped again. "We won't let you pass," yelled Chiboques. "You must come to our village."

David labored to walk to the front of his Makalolos. He turned to them. "We are going ahead, men. Don't fight unless they fight first." He walked forward, and leveled his rifle on a man who seemed to be the leader. He yelled, "I could kill you easily." He pointed to the sky. "But I fear God!"

The man stepped forward. "I am Ionga Panza. I, too, fear to kill. We only want you to come to our village."

David couldn't resist the man's appeal. And they all proceeded to the village where Ionga Panza presented the travelers with a goat, then demanded an ox and a tusk for payment. To make matters worse, slave traders showed up with firearms and took the side of the Chiboques. So David surrendered one ox and one tusk. Ionga Panza refused the first ox because its tail had been severed in an accident; to the Chiboques that meant the ox was bewitched.

When David parleyed with his Makalolos in the forest after they left the village, they were more discouraged than they had ever been. Several wanted to start back immediately.

"You can't go," pleaded David. "The Portuguese settlements are only a few days away! We're almost there."

One of the Makalolos spoke for the others. "We want to go back now before we lose everything."

David felt like Columbus. The same thing had happened to him. Just as his goal seemed within reach there was a mutiny on his ship. Guided by God's hand, he had asked the crew for a few more days. The crew agreed to a deadline. Just before the deadline arrived, Columbus discovered an entire new world! David must trust God, just as Columbus had.

"Today is the 24th of March, men. Give me one more week. And cut off the tails of our last four oxen immediately," said David, amazed he had not thought of it sooner.

"Cut off? . . ." Mashauana laughed. "Yes, cut their tails off. We'll surely lose no more oxen."

The Makalolos agreed to continue. They seemed to find relief in the trick to save their oxen. And David tried not to feel too much pleasure in seeing the solution applied to Sinbad. Six days later the caravan reached a ledge and looked one thousand feet down into a colossal valley.

"This must be the valley of the Quango," said David.

The other side of the valley could not be seen. A blanket of dark green forest stretched north to the horizon. In meander bends of the river were light green meadows of grass. The valley of the Quango seemed paradise.

The descent was so steep that many slopes were bare red soil. David could not ride Sinbad on such slopes. David was so weak Makalolos had to hold him up as he stumbled down the slope on foot or he would have toppled into space. His doctor's mind knew he was almost dead from river fever. He was a bag of bones. Surely God wouldn't let him die just before victory.

When they reached the valley floor, David saw the Quango was very muddy, a circumstance not seen by him in any African river before. The river itself was one hundred fifty yards wide and very deep. The men would need canoes. They worked their way toward a village situated far back from the river.

The travelers were met by a local chief. "I am Sansawe of the Bashinjes." Sansawe was young. He wore a conical cap which pointed straight back from his head. His beard was forked.

"Why is your village so far off the river?" asked David.

"Because the river swarms with poisonous snakes. You must get our help to cross. I see you have tusks. I want them."

"We have more than tusks," said David.

"Good. Let me see everything you possess," said Sansawe boldly.

David showed him the mirror and the compass. He had never liked to create the impression with natives that he was supernatural. But today when he saw the fear grow in Sansawe's eyes, he fed that fear. Soon Sansawe was sure David was bewitched. He couldn't escape to his village fast enough.

"We'll go farther down the river to find canoes," David told his Makalolos.

The chief from the next village also met them, demanding tribute. Would this evil never end? Somehow they had to get themselves across the Quango. "Please God," David prayed, "end this misery."

"Look!" said Mashauana.

Mystically, a man approached them. He wore a military uniform! "I am Cypriano di Abreu," the man said in Portuguese. With gestures the soldier explained he was on this side of the Quango to buy beeswax.

David knew enough Portuguese to tell the soldier he wanted to cross the Quango. Soon Cypriano, who was a sergeant, arranged their crossing. On the opposite shore, Cypriano said, "You are now in the domain of the Portuguese. The natives on this side of the Quango are Bangalas, our subjects."

After they reached a small outpost of adobe buildings, David produced a letter of recommendation he had carried with him ever since he left Cape Town in 1852. The letter was written by a powerful Portuguese official. After that, Cypriano treated him like royalty. David learned they were still three hundred miles from the Atlantic Ocean, but the trip was only tedious, not dangerous.

Six days later they departed, rested and well fed, up the west slope of the valley. In three days, they reached Cassange, a Portuguese station with several dozen houses. Every Portuguese soldier stationed there was also a trader, an inducement to live in such a remote area. Again David produced his letter. On April 16, 1854, David celebrated Easter Sunday with the locals. Bangalas participated. There were no priests in Cassange. This reinforced David's opinion that the mere presence of Europeans practicing Christianity was enough to make Africans want to live in Christ.

If only the Portuguese did not practice slavery. In many ways, they were more enlightened than the English. Many Portuguese soldiers had Bangala wives and could not have loved their offspring more. In southern Africa such half-breeds were despised by the English and Boers. David had seen this wonderful attitude of the Portuguese about race before—in Rio de Janeiro.

The commander, Captain Neva, entertained David. To one who had lived on manioc and scraps of beef for weeks on end, the feast was fit for a king. Captain Neva had cookies from America, beer from England, and wines and preserved fruits from Portugal.

One morning Mashauana came to David, breathless. "We want to trade Sekeletu's tusks here."

"Why not wait? We can probably get more goods for

them at Luanda on the seashore."

"Maybe not." Mashauana took David to a trader. "Tell Doctor Livingstone," he said in Bantu to the trader, "what he can get for one tusk."

"Two muskets, three barrels of gunpowder, and sixty yards of English cotton."

David was astonished. "One tusk is worth so much here?"

No wonder trade flourished in western Africa. Was ivory so precious here? He hadn't known. He thought the main commerce was in slaves. This was very heartening. The Makalolos had almost been giving away their ivory. He had seen a chief trade two tusks for one musket. If the Africans in the interior could trade their tusks near the oceans, they not only could buy abundant goods but there would be less incentive to deal in slaves.

Soon he was trading. Before he knew it he had traded all three of Sekeletu's remaining tusks for that trader's goods and one horse for Sekeletu. His men were very pleased. But David had a problem: His Makalolos wanted to go back now.

"But I can't get to the coast without your help," said David.

"We will be captured. The Portuguese allow slavery."

"I will fight for you, just as I promised you back among the Chiboques."

Reluctantly, his men came with him.

As they proceeded, David was disturbed. He was having difficulty making geographical measurements. The procedure itself was extremely complicated, so much so that some men could not learn it at all. But David had had no difficulty before. He also noticed he could not remember some names now. He was a doctor. The conclusion was unmistakable. His illness was grave. He was so anemic his mind was failing.

After a succession of military posts, they reached Luanda

on the coast. Civilization staggered his Makalolos. Luandans made buildings that deserved to be called mountains with caves in them. The inhabitants burned black stones for heat. Ships in the harbor held entire villages and carried so much cargo it took weeks to unload. The Atlantic Ocean defied description because it stretched to the horizon, even if one climbed high into the foothills. And there were thousands of black slaves inhabiting Luanda!

But his Makalolos saw something else. David Livingstone was a source of wonder to these Luandans. He had trekked from where? From Cape Town through central Africa? Impossible. He looked at death's door. The English consul, Edmund Gabriel, hurriedly took him into his own home. David was confined to bed. Doctors visited to diagnose his illness. He received the governor, the Catholic bishop, and every person of influence in Luanda. English officers left their warships to visit him.

David's Makalolos began to relax. David seemed powerful enough to protect them, even after he suffered a severe relapse. He was helpless. He prayed for the safety of his men. Soon he learned in his stupor that his Makalolos were remarkable. They went into the foothills to cut firewood and lug it back to sell in Luanda. They hired out to unload coal ships from England. Praise the Lord for his men's industry. This would benefit them greatly because now they had their own money to buy goods to take back to their homeland.

David fought to recover. There was not one European who did not advise him to return to England as soon as possible. And his answer was always the same: "I must get my Makalolos back to their home."

This loyalty struck a chord among all men. He heard unguarded whispers about his courage. *If only they all knew,* he prayed, *that true courage comes from Christ.* What did they think of him deep in their hearts? Did they think he was a fool?

The bishop came again. To David's men, he presented smart red and blue suits, caps, and blankets. He gave David a very decorous officer's uniform for Sekeletu. He also gave Sekeletu a horse, complete with bridle and saddle! The Bishop said David was doing something very special with the Africans in the interior. His work should be encouraged in every way.

David began to recover. He had deteriorated to the absolute limit—and lived, thanks to God. He realized no letters from anyone had found him at Luanda. Who had believed he would be there anyway? He felt well enough to fret over Mary's condition. If only he knew how she and the children were doing. He wrote long letters to her. He wrote letters to all his correspondents, as well. After four months he was ready to travel again.

The Bishop continued to astound him. "I've secured twenty porters to help you and your Makalolos on the journey," he told David.

"That's not necessary."

But David was wrong. He needed the extra porters. When his departure became known, they were inundated by gifts from the Portuguese: donkeys, beads, cotton goods, ammunition, and muskets. Every one of his men would return armed.

"Tributes will be very reasonable on the return trip," promised Mashauana.

On September 20, 1854, David departed for the country of Sekeletu. The return trip was riddled with bouts of fever. David had recorded his own bouts of fever as rigorously as his geographical measurement of longitude and latitude. He had suffered well over two dozen attacks since his first attack on the Sesheke almost one year ago. Many Makalolos were also laid low by river fever. Often the caravan had to stop for several days.

All through Portuguese territory, he wrote Mary letters. In a letter written in October, he revealed his strategy:

> *It occurs to me, my dearest Mary, that if I send you a note from different parts on the way through this colony, some of them will surely reach you; and if they carry any of the affection I bear to you in their composition, they will not fail to comfort you. . . .*
>
> *I remained a short time longer in Loanda than was actually required to set me on my legs, in longing expectation of a letter from you. . . . Give my love to all the children. . . . How happy I shall be to meet them and you again! I hope a letter from you may be waiting for me at Zambesi. Love to all the children. How tall is Zouga [Oswell]? Accept the assurance of my unabated love. . . .*

After David crossed the Quango and left the hospitable Portuguese, he tried to skirt the troublesome Chiboque chiefs by traveling forty miles farther north. But he encountered many of the same chiefs anyway, with the same haggling over tribute. Several times a battle seemed unavoidable, but at the last second the crisis evaporated. Once David had to strike one of his own men over the head with his pistol butt to keep the man from shooting a Chiboque in anger after the crisis had been resolved.

In June of 1855 near the village of Katema, he passed Dilolo, a triangular lake about eight miles long and two miles wide. One river drained the lake to the north into the river systems of the Kasai. When he reached the south end of the lake, he was shocked to find a river emptying the lake south into the river systems of the Sesheke. The lake was like a fountain welling up on a ridge and spewing water into lowlands on both sides. Water from this one small lake actually flowed both to the Atlantic Ocean and the Indian Ocean. Oh, marvelous Africa! He wanted to study the remarkable phenomenon but began vomiting blood. As he did so often, he surged onward as if that would defeat his sickness.

The African wilderness was not a land that indulged relaxation. Death came unexpectedly: from drowning, from fever, from war, or from animals. Men and women David had met during the trip from the Barotse Valley to Luanda were dead by the time he returned on the same route: Cypriano's mother, Nyamoana's husband, Mpololo's wife and daughter, and several others. Even the ox Sinbad died from tsetse bites—near Manenko's village—after plodding three thousand cantankerous miles. Yet David lost not one Makalolo from his own party!

Praise the Lord. Surely God was looking over them.

But in Africa danger was ever present and death could come unexpectedly. . . .

THIRTEEN

Yes, danger was never far away in Africa.

Back in the good game country of the Balondas, David's caravan left the Sesheke River to hunt in open grassland. David shot a zebra near a herd of buffalo. The wounded zebra bolted away, pursued by Makalolos. David watched the herd of buffalo warily. In his experience the buffalo was the most diabolical of all African game. A buffalo would flee into the brush, actually double back on its own trail, crouch on its knees near the trail, and wait to ambush a hunter.

"Never underestimate a buffalo," he muttered as he eyed the herd.

The buffalo charges in a ponderous gallop that can almost overtake a horse. One of the most terrifying sights in Africa is the charge of a buffalo on the open plain. One might dodge a rhino, but one could rarely ever dodge a buffalo. It charged head down, so that the skull was covered by a thick armor plate of horn. A successful head shot was impossible. . . .

"My Makalolos seem miles away," said David as he realized

how alone he was. He squinted. In the distance was a haze of dust, probably raised by his Makalolos as they ran after the zebra he wounded.

Closer to David, a buffalo separated itself from the herd. The beast was studying him. David glanced around him for refuge. There were no trees near him. The river was too far away. The buffalo broke into a canter. It raised its tail like a cavalry guidon.

It was charging!

David reloaded both barrels. He said to the sky, "I will wait until the last second to shoot. Then I will dive for the ground. The rest is up to You, Lord."

David edged to the side so that a small bush tens of yards away from him was directly in the buffalo's path. The black form grew and took on sound. Seconds away from David, the buffalo swerved to miss the bush, exposing its shoulder. David fired both barrels. Then he dove. *Please God,* he prayed, *let it be the right direction.*

The ground vibrated from the monster's hooves. David clutched handfuls of grass and waited for the horns to pitch him. But the rumbling diminished. David looked up. The buffalo ran on toward the river. Praise the Lord. David stood up. The beast reached the river, stopped, and swirled in confusion. Then it crumpled to its knees and toppled over. David reloaded and walked to within twenty yards. He threw a stick against the animal. The buffalo was dead.

One of his Makalolos approached. "The zebra got away. We ran all that way for nothing. Oh, I see you shot a buffalo. You might have told us." The man pulled his knife and nonchalantly started butchering.

By August of 1855, they were cruising down the Sesheke River in canoes again. David was lost in thought. His faculties were almost back to normal. He was pondering the geology of southern Africa. It was an ancient landmass, almost flat everywhere, with very minor mountain building. That's why it had such peculiar features as lakes draining into rivers, whereas everywhere else in the world the opposite was true. He had talked to very old men in the villages. They maintained long oral histories. No African between the latitudes of 7 degrees and 27 degrees south of the equator had ever felt an earthquake. That just confirmed what he knew about the flat stable landmass of Africa.

At Linyanti, a massive celebration erupted. "You're alive!" exclaimed Sekeletu.

David and his party had been considered long dead by Sekeletu and his counselors. Now they held a colossal kotla with hours of speeches. Sekeletu was astounded that not one of his twenty-seven Makalolos was lost. How was it possible on such a dangerous journey? It cemented the perception of David as being blessed. Gifts from the west abounded: horses, donkeys, clothing, ammunition, and guns. Sekeletu quickly donned his officer's uniform.

The kotla was thrown into turmoil, too. Ivory could buy so much in the west! And Makalolos had much ivory. So many opportunities! Some wanted to relocate up the Barotse Valley right away to be nearer to the western markets. Others argued they must remain here in the feverish swamps to discourage the Zulus from attacking. David did not discourage their speculation. After all, he wanted trade. No one was talking about trading with slave traders anymore. It was wonderful.

At last, Sekeletu spoke, "I would like to go up the Barotse Valley to live. This new trade route is very good for us. Livingstone is going east now, but he will return and open a mission here."

A complication had jumped out of David's past. He had never found a satisfactory location for a mission. He had forgotten that goal. Trade had become so much more important to him. Even now he could think of little else but exploring the Seseheke River downstream, hopefully east to the Indian Ocean. But he forced himself to think about Sekeletu's wish. Yes, he could start a mission up the Barotse Valley. Perhaps near Shinte. The location was not ideal. River fever was still prevalent. But he could survive there. And Mary was up to it. But not the children.

He told Sekeletu, "I will write the London Missionary Society with suggestions. But next, I must go east. I want to leave in a few days. I am very anxious to see my family."

"The winter is just ending," protested Sekeletu. "Surely you can't travel in the hot season."

"We will travel on a great river. It's not like crossing the Kalahari wilderness."

But it was very hot already. It was over 100 degrees in the shade. The night cooled only to a steamy 90 degrees. David stayed with Sekeletu until the first rain broke the heat. In spite of the hot season, he was going to leave. It was his old problem. He couldn't lose years waiting around for the seasons to mesh with his plans.

In November, Sekeletu and two hundred men escorted him down the Seseheke River. Sekeletu supplied David with twelve oxen and food. Many tusks were in the caravan's cargo for sale downriver. The young chief picked Sekwebu for David's guide down the Seseheke. Sekwebu had been captured by Zulus as a small boy. He escaped but had grown up far down the Seseheke River by the Portuguese settlement of Tete. He knew both banks of the Seseheke for hundreds of miles between Tete and the kingdom of Sekeletu.

As they neared a place called Mosioatunya, David began to understand why Sekeletu was so excited. The phrase *mosi oa tunya* meant "smoke makes sound there." In the distance five columns of white vapor billowed off the river into the clouds. As the travelers got closer to the clouds, a pervasive whisper grew into a roar. They canoed to an island and walked to the end. Then they crawled onto an overhang.

"It's stupendous," said David, his words smothered by the roar. The Sesheke River, two thousand yards wide from bank to bank, cascaded over a ledge into what seemed a boiling cauldron. The water fell three hundred feet. "I shall name it Victoria Falls after the young queen."

Later he wrote:

> *The whole body of water rolls clear over, quite unbroken; but after a descent of ten or more feet the entire mass becomes like a huge sheet of driven snow. Pieces of water leap off it in the form of comets with tails streaming behind, till the whole snowy sheet becomes myriads of rushing, leaping, aqueous comets. . . .*

Sekeletu left him with 114 Makalolos, most of whom were carrying ivory for trade. South of the river lurked the notorious Zulus; so David and his caravan ascended a plateau north of the river. Cooler drier air soothed them. Game abounded. The soil appeared suitable for crops like coffee and corn.

"This is the best location I've seen for a mission since I came to Sekeletu," he mused. Then he was startled as he realized that was two and half years ago! He had had no contact whatever with Mary and the children for even longer than that. *God forgive me,* he prayed.

They were in the land of the Batoka. David was not fond

of Batokas. Batokas were in the realm of Sekeletu's Makalolos, but they were the most recalcitrant of his subjects. Even
the great Sebitoane had failed to stop their disgusting habit of
men and women alike knocking out their upper front teeth.
As a consequence, the lower teeth seemed to project grotesquely. And their greeting repulsed David. They would lie on
their backs, rolling side to side while slapping their thighs,
and yelling *kina bomba!* But he began to wonder if his constant illness from river fever was not making him intolerant of
native ways.

Some of his own party of Makalolos were Batokas. They
had no grasp of tact. When they entered one village a Batoka
in David's party blurted, "I killed a man here once." Otherwise, native Batokas were friendly, supplying the party with
corn and ground nuts. No tribute was demanded because of
the presence of Sekeletu's men.

Hunting in the plateau north of the Sesheke River was
unsurpassed. Buffalo and elephants were killed to provide
royal quantities of meat for the men. At one spot where they
descended into a green valley, David saw so many zebras, buffalo, and elephants—and the animals were so tame—that the
image overwhelmed him. This was paradise. It pained him
deeply to think such glimpses into paradise would pass from
the earth. In his heart, he knew the arrival of guns into the
interior plus the value of ivory would destroy paradise.

"Am I not an agent of that change?" he asked God.

The trip was a succession of tribes and friendly villages until
early in 1856 when the caravan encountered Chief Mburuma
along the great river. The source of the trouble was another
white man, an Italian, who with the help of fifty slaves tried to
establish himself as some kind of chief in the area. The man
was killed and now all white men were suspect to Chief

Mburuma. David smoothed things over, but he sensed once again he was in territory like that of the Chiboques, beyond the influence of Sekeletu. Every day was filled with danger now.

They passed Zumbo, the site of a former Portuguese outpost. Houses and walls of sandstone had crumbled. It was the best site yet for a mission. Sekwebu told David the Portuguese men in Zumbo had disintegrated long before the sandstone. Instead of trying to grow coffee, wheat, or corn, the Portuguese colonists traded in slaves. And the natives drove them away.

From the village of Chief Mpende, war parties approached, dancing and threatening with spears. But David had dealt with many difficult chiefs. Always he displayed power in firearms while acting very calm and reasonable. Soon Mpende calmed, too, even recommending that David cross to the south side of the river because the journey to Tete was easier that way. David's party was very suspicious. River crossings were notorious for double crosses. Many a party had been split up during a crossing and slaughtered.

"It was a favorite trick of Sebitoane's," Sekwebu told David nervously.

This crossing was uneventful. David bypassed the river to find easier traveling in uplands. They were on constant alert for Zulus. One Makalolo died of fever; one vanished in an area notorious for lions. And the closer the party got to Tete in the colony of Mozambique, the sicker David and the other Makalolos became from fever. Mozambique was known for its unhealthy outposts on the fever-ridden Zambesi River.

David did not make it to Tete. On March 2nd of 1856, he collapsed in his tent, brought down by fever. His mind was muddled again. Only days before he could not remember a simple method of measuring the width of the river with his sextant. Now from his tent, he sent Sekwebu ahead to Tete with letters of recommendation he carried from the bishop in Luanda.

Within hours, soldiers arrived to escort David to Tete. Just the sight of help revived him. He walked the remaining eight miles to Tete to be met by Major Sicard. Then he collapsed, an invalid again among the Portuguese.

In his fever he asked his host, "Is this the Zambesi River that empties into the Indian Ocean?"

"Certainly," shrugged Major Sicard.

David's hope was realized. Sekeletu's Sesheke River that went all the way up into the Barotse Valley to Lake Dilolo really did go all the way to the Indian Ocean as the Zambesi River. He questioned the Major about the one hundred miles of Zambesi he had bypassed by using Mpende's shortcut south of the river. The Major had heard old-timers say there were some rapids called Kebrabasa in that stretch. They were rapids though, not cataracts.

Of the four thousand inhabitants of Tete only a few hundred were free. In David's mind slavery was the reason the Portuguese had lost their opportunity to open up Africa. They sat here on a great river highway that reached into the very heart of Africa and did nothing but trade in slaves. Their obsession with slavery worried him now. The Portuguese might not be so friendly to English merchants trying to ply their honest trade on the Zambesi.

David was well enough to travel in April. All but sixteen of Sekeletu's Makalolos were to remain in Tete, free men under the protection of the Portuguese. The sixteen Makalolos and several Portuguese soldiers accompanied him down the Zambesi in canoes. Halfway to the port of Quilimane, David released all the Makalolos. Sekwebu begged to come with him to the Indian Ocean. He relented. In May of 1856, they arrived in Quilimane.

Colonel Nunes was his host. David could tell from the pity in the Colonel's eyes, he must have looked pathetic. David felt closer to death than he ever had felt in his life. "You have letters from England here, Doctor Livingstone," said Colonel Nunes to cheer his guest.

"At last! A letter from Mary," cried David as he pawed through the letters. But not one was from Mary. It was crushing. He looked at Colonel Nunes. "I'll read the others later. Before I do, I must make a request. In case of my death, please sell the ivory we brought and give the proceeds to Sekwebu."

"But you will recover," protested his host unconvincingly. "The reason I have letters for you, Doctor Livingstone, is because English warships have been stopping here off and on, asking for you. . . ." His face was sour.

"Does that disturb you, sir?"

"I'm afraid I have some bad news. Some of the Englishmen from the brigantine *Dart* were drowned on a sandbar off the river's mouth last year trying to reach our port in a rowboat."

"No!"

"Unfortunately, it's true. Two officers and five seamen."

"On account of me?"

His host ignored that question. "Englishmen from the *Frolic* left this for you as well as the letters." David was too numb to see what he had in a box. He stumbled off to bed. Seven men had died because of him.

After a fitful sleep, he opened the box to find medical supplies. He wasted no time taking quinine. Then he opened a letter from Roderick Murchison, a well-known English geologist. Murchison raved that David's trip to Luanda was "the greatest triumph in geographical research. . .in our times." David's only use for praise was the hope that it advanced his missionary work to save souls. Otherwise, praise was nothing but fodder for pride. And the deaths of the seven seamen weighed on his mind.

The next letter he opened was from the London publisher John Murray. Murray wrote that he was interested in publishing a book about David's adventures in Africa. He would pay all expenses involved and give David part of the profits. It sounded much too good to be true.

"Can there really be any interest in such a book?" David asked himself. "No. Probably the enthusiastic Roderick Murchison pressured Murray into writing a letter of interest."

The last letter was from the London Missionary Society. He opened the letter, determined to resist their praise, and read:

> *The Directors, while yielding to none in their appreciation of the objects upon which, for some years past, your energies have been concentrated, or in admiration of the zeal, intrepidity, and success with which they have been carried out, are nevertheless restricted in their power of aiding plans connected only remotely with the spread of the gospel. . . .*

"Connected only remotely with the spread of the gospel?"

David slammed the letter down. Had he read it correctly? Yes. They were condemning his activity. They understood nothing of what he was doing. They were pleading lack of funds, when in fact he had spent his own salary for several years. Only the Lord knew what poor Mary and the children were living on. Even years ago he spent his own salary to build the missions at Chonuane and Kolobeng. And the Missionary Society had spent almost nothing on his exploration in the last few years. He closed his eyes and prayed to the Lord to quash his bitterness. But when he opened his eyes, the world looked very sour. So this was a preview of what awaited him in England.

At the bottom of the letter was the news that Mary and the children were doing fine. Praise God for that. By the time the *Frolic* returned in July to anchor offshore, David had conquered his depression. At least his family was all right. As always he had written a flood of letters to his correspondents, even the Directors of the London Missionary Society, calmly explaining how his exploration had to precede the spread of the gospel.

As David prepared to leave Quilimane with men from the *Frolic*, Sekwebu begged to go with him. "Let me die at your feet," he cried.

David liked Sekwebu very much. He was intelligent, tactful, and resourceful. He had been the essential man along the Zambesi. "Come along then."

The boat ride down the Zambesi and over the sand bars to the *Frolic* was savage. Waves battered the small boat and swept over the passengers. Veteran crewmen bailed water furiously, making no pretense of hiding their fear. Seven had died on this trip previously.

Sekwebu was terrified. "Is this the way you go in this boat?" he kept repeating.

The *Frolic*, a brig so large she carried sixteen cannon and 130 seamen, was rolling in a violent sea. The men in the boat barely made it aboard. David felt alien to the Englishmen. They gaped when he spoke. His halting English was so rusty he must have spoken with a very peculiar accent. But Sekwebu suffered far more. His eyes were glazed with terror. The ship was a death trap.

For one month, Sekwebu tried to adjust as they sailed the

open ocean. When the *Frolic* stopped at an island Sekwebu tried to abandon ship. David reasoned with him. The captain said Sekwebu was going mad from the sea; he had seen the signs before. Sekwebu must be shackled and confined. David insisted that would be too harsh and prevailed. But Sekwebu did go mad that night. He leaped into the sea, never to be seen again.

"Oh, why did I yield to my own better judgement and bring him? And why did I not listen to the captain?" David lamented to God. "Sekwebu's precious life is on my hands now. What else can go wrong?"

He left the *Frolic* and steamed through the Red Sea on the *Candida*. At Cairo, David finally had a letter from home. His father, Neil, was dead! He died just months before David was to return to England. The mounting heartbreaks were almost too much for David. He felt like Job. Would the suffering ever end? Surely his first meeting with Mary would make up for all the pain. Surely she and the children were all right.

"Aren't they?" he suddenly cried, startled at the thought.

FOURTEEN

Surely Mary and the children were all right. David was very anxious to get back to England now. His steamship was delayed at Marseilles due to a broken engine shaft, so he left it and crossed France on the train. In December of 1856 he crossed the channel to England.

"Mary is not here!" he cried in alarm as he docked at Dover. No one was there!

Had Mary not heard of his change of plans? Or had something happened to her? Perhaps she waited for him at Southampton where his steamship from Egypt was supposed to dock. *Please God, let my family be all right,* he prayed as the coach hurtled him toward Southampton.

"Yes! I see them."

Mary was waiting where his steamship was supposed to have docked. David was overcome with joy. As he hugged Mary, the children withdrew from him. They had not seen him in four years. That night, Mary had to express her thoughts with a poem she had written for the occasion:

A hundred thousand welcomes, and it's time for you
      to come
From the far land of the foreigner, to your country and
      your home.
Oh, long as we were parted, ever since you went away,
I never passed an easy night, or knew an easy day.

Do you think I would reproach you with the sorrows
      that I bore?
Since the sorrow is all over now I have you here
      once more,
And there's nothing but the gladness and the love
      within my heart,
And the hope so sweet and certain that again we'll
      never part.

A hundred thousand welcomes! how my heart is
      gushing o'er
With the love and joy and wonder thus to see your face
      once more.
How did I live without you these long long years of woe?
      It seems as if 'twould kill me to be parted from
      you now.

You'll never part me, darling, there's a promise in
      your eye;
I may tend you while I'm living, you will watch me
      when I die;
And if death but kindly lead me to the blessed home
      on high,
What a hundred thousand welcomes will await you in
      the sky!

David hugged the children. Robert and Mary were ten and nine, quite proper young English children. Thomas and Zouga, seven and five, were not yet molded, still unruly and outspoken. What a joy to see them all healthy.

It was only later that David realized the depths of misery Mary's poem revealed. Mary had truly suffered. He would get to the bottom of it. From the children he was shocked to learn that Mary had not adjusted to living with his father and mother in Hamilton. They had not even been on speaking terms after the first six months.

He learned from Mary that after she had left the children in Hamilton, she drifted from one cheap apartment to another, in Hackney, in Manchester, in Kendal, in Epsom. Occasionally, she stayed with friends of her father, Robert Moffat. She subsisted on tiny handouts from the Missionary Society.

David was shocked. "How can I ever make it up to you?"

And what was he going to do about the London Missionary Society? His mother-in-law's letters from Kuruman were small comfort. She hid nothing from David. Some missionaries in South Africa ridiculed him as a wandering fool.

He wrote back angrily to denounce "those so-called missionaries to the heathen, who never march into real heathen territory, and quiet their consciences by opposing their do-nothingism to my blundering do-somethingism!"

What was David going to do? Anger did not soothe his guilt and his sense of failure. Sixteen hard years in Africa and what did his own family have to show for it?

When David was asked to take Mary to a meeting of the Royal Geographic Society three days later, he began to get nervous. Yes, he heard it whispered, it was in his honor. Once again he was the recipient of their Gold Medal. The monetary reward was a token amount. When he arrived, he was surprised to see the meeting overflowing with dukes and earls and the haughtiest members of London society. He was cheered to see his old friends Cotton Oswell and Captain Thomas Steele.

"They seem to have gone to quite a lot of bother, Mary," he murmured. He wore blue trousers and a black coat with long tails over a white shirt and black bow tie. "Good thing I dressed for it." He longed to tug on his gold-banded blue cap.

Roderick Murchison stood and spoke on and on about the accomplishments of the great missionary David Livingstone. The renowned biologist Richard Owen had tears in his eyes as he told how David, almost dead from fever, brought him a rare coiled tusk from Africa.

David became more and more uncomfortable. What were they making of him? If they only knew all the days he had squirmed and groaned and vomited with river fever. If they only knew how his bad judgement had killed Sekwebu. David was no hero. The only important thing was finding a route for the gospel.

Finally, David himself stood, self-conscious of his rough appearance: dark-skinned, emaciated, face deeply furrowed from worry. His English words of thanks were halting, unsure, and thickly accented. "I am only doing my duty as a missionary in opening up a part of Africa to the sympathy of Christ. Captain Steele or Mister Cotton Oswell could have done as well as I did. And besides, I am only just now buckling on my armor for the good fight. I have no right to boast of anything. I will not boast until the last slave in Africa is free, and Africa is open to honest trade and the light of Christianity. . . ."

After the meeting Murchison took him aside. "When I first saw you, Livingstone, I thought you were as broken down as an old cart horse. 'No more Africa for him,' I thought. But how your eyes burned just then as you talked! You are too modest. I have no doubt whatever that you are the only one in England who could have done what you did in Africa."

"Not so, sir," replied David with complete conviction.

"Naturally," said Murchison, "I would never wish you to fall away from your Missionary Society. But societies are more limited than governments when it comes to funding exploration. . . ."

"I'm meeting with the Missionary Society tomorrow," said David, not sure how to reply.

"Good," said Murchison. "I hope you are pleased with the meeting. After all, you know exactly what must be done to serve Christ. However, if you not pleased with the meeting, perhaps there is another agency that would allow you to do exactly what you know must be done to open up Africa. I urge you to contact me immediately. I know the Earl of Clarendon intimately. He is the Foreign Secretary under Lord Palmerston, the Prime Minister."

David was stunned. What was Murchison doing? First, some talk of a book. Now was he hinting of some kind of commission for the government? Was Murchison all bluff?

The next day, much to David's satisfaction, Mary was also feted with him by the London Missionary Society. They praised her for her patient endurance. But as David sat and listened, he could not escape a feeling of bitterness. While he spent his own meager salary on Africa, Mary had suffered for lack of funds. Now they heaped praise on David, thick and gooey. Again he found himself sour. Yes, he had accomplished much, but it seemed only because he leaped ahead and then told the Society later what he had done. Those brothers who waited on permission stagnated for years.

He thanked them for sixteen years of patience with a missionary who strained the limits. He was sincere. He knew he was very trying to such conservative men. But as he studied their pasty well-fed faces that rarely saw the sun and remembered the unrelenting woes of Africa, anger crept into his heart. He finished with a petulant regret that his ventures were seen as "only a tempting of Providence" by "the weaker brethren."

Afterwards Mary said, "David, such a remark is expected in salty letters between friends. Even my mother writes such things. But do you think it is wise to talk that way with the Directors?"

"I feel guided by an Unseen Hand. Perhaps the Society is not the best way to bring Christ to Africa."

"David! You don't mean that."

A few days later, the publisher John Murray visited him. "When do we start, Doctor Livingstone?"

Was Murchison right? David asked bluntly, "Do you mean there may be interest in such a technical book?"

"Didn't you hear what they said about you at the Royal Geographic Society?"

"Yes. But geographers are only human, Mister Murray. They too need to create enthusiasm to generate funds for their Society. I realize there is some interest among the gentry."

"You are so down to earth, Doctor. Trust me, sir. I am so sure your book will repay me a hundredfold I will give you two-thirds of the profits rather than the customary one-third. When can you start?"

"I must visit my mother and sisters in Scotland first."

And that was where David went next. Both Janet and Agnes still lived with his mother. They both taught school. John had immigrated to Canada. And Charles was a pastor in America. David had never been in their new home in Hamilton where his father died so recently.

"Tell me about Father," he asked.

Janet told him, "He knew he was dying. He wanted very much to see you again but said the will of the Lord must be done. His last words were 'But I think I'll know in heaven whatever is worth knowing about David. When you see him, tell him that.'"

"Praise the Lord for such a father," said David. And he knew there were those in Scotland and England who praised David not at all. He had neglected his own children to spread the gospel to God's black children. Remarks made by his sisters only reinforced his suspicions that Mary and the children had spent a wretched four years. Couldn't the Missionary Society have been responsive to their needs?

Days later on January 12, 1857, at a Board meeting of the London Missionary Society in London, David challenged the Directors. In his own mind, it was an ultimatum. He proposed two new missions: one in the land of the Zulus administered by Robert Moffat and one in the land of Sekeletu's Makalolos administered by him.

"Of course, you and Mary will reside in the mission among the Makalolos, won't you?" asked a Director.

"Perhaps," said David evasively. Six months ago his answer would have been an enthusiastic yes, but the suffering of Mary still bothered him. How could the Society take so much for granted? Were the wives of these Directors suffering from tropical fevers? Were any of their children buried in Africa?

The Directors convened the meeting with no decision. David resented that. It meant they would discuss it among themselves privately. Hadn't he earned the right to argue his case right up to the verdict? Would his proposals be defeated in secret? Their elite and undemocratic procedures bothered him more and more. He reminded himself they were only men after all.

He had been staying at Doctor Bennett's house, but now he moved his family to a house in Chelsea. He explained to Doctor Bennett that he would be working full time on his book. Mary liked her new home. She no longer felt she was living on charity. And David had severed one more tie with the Society.

He was told in late January that the Society had approved his proposal for the two missions, but first they had to write Robert Moffat. It might take awhile to draft the letter into precise language. *Not to mention,* thought David, *the time it will take for the letter to reach Moffat in Kuruman. Not to mention the time it will take Moffat to travel to the Zulus to get their permission. Not to mention the time it will take Moffat to write back to the Society, with his suggested revisions. What year might the proposals be finally approved? 1859? 1860? 1861?*

The next day, he wrote a letter to Lord Clarendon. *Would the Foreign Office,* he asked, *be at all interested in funding an expedition to explore the Zambesi River—in the very near future?*

About the same time, he received a newspaper from Cape Town. He could scarcely believe his eyes. A banquet honored him in Cape Town in November of 1856. On the occasion the Governor said:

> *I think no man of the present day is more deserving than David Livingstone—a man whom we, indeed, can hardly regard as belonging to any particular age or time, but who belongs to the whole Christian epoch, possessing all those great qualities of mind and that resolute desire at all risks to spread the gospel. . . . Indeed, that man must be regarded as almost of apostolic character. . . .*

Good Lord! thought David. *That can't be me.* He read the remarks of the Colonial Secretary:

> *I am convinced that Livingstone's name will live amongst the first heroes and the first benefactors of our race.*

No! That's too much. Such praise was so undeserved. Were other men so little? The man representing the London Missionary Society said:

> *If ever there was a man who, by realizing the obligations of his sacred calling as a Christian missionary, and intelligently comprehending its object, sought to pursue it to a successful issue, such a man is Doctor Livingstone.*

David almost believed that flattery, except he had not brought it to a successful issue. What had he accomplished? He was proud, however, when he read the words of Maclear, the Royal Astronomer of Cape Town:

> *What this man has done is unprecedented. You could go to any point across the entire continent, along Livingstone's track, and feel certain of your position.*

I'll accept that praise from the Royal Astronomer, thought David. Oh, the pain David had endured on some feverish days to take those laborious measurements. And he reflected on Cape Town. Could this be the same city that had stalled him back in 1852? Could this be the same city that balked at selling him supplies? How quickly men were swayed one way or the other. Doubt grew in his heart. All this praise could so quickly turn to scorn. And how could he be a failure one day and be a hero the next? He felt guilty making plans with the British government. But the Missionary Society was so slow. David had only one life to live. And a man must strike for Christ when the time is right. Could the time ever be more right than now?

At Chelsea, he plunged into his book, keeping his antennae up for developments from the Missionary Society or the Foreign Office. He pored over his thick journals and condensed parts of them and expanded other parts of them. In his own fashion, he was trying to do the work of two years in six months.

Roderick Murchison took him to meet Lord Clarendon. The Foreign Secretary was effusive. What did David need? What title did he want for his commission? David seemed reluctant to accept such gratuities. Lord Clarendon snapped, "Good heavens, Doctor, I'm not doing you a favor. You are doing England a favor. You are a man who *gets things done.* Now if you want to save all those African souls as speedily as possible, please send me a detailed proposal so I can show it to the prime minister."

What an opportunity! It seemed David could ask for anything. But could he leave the Mission Society? What would people think? He immediately inquired as to the progress of the letter to Robert Moffat. He was told they were working on it. . . .

By March 19, the Mission Society still had not drafted the letter. So David sent his official proposal to Lord Clarendon. Later Murchison told him it was well received. "The Foreign Secretary is off and running," he added.

"To whom?" joked David.

"Prince Albert." ·

"The Prince?" David was surprised.

"To attend to the sensitive relationship with Portugal. You are the one who told us no expedition could ever start up the Zambesi River without their approval. The first thing the prime minister must do is ask Prince Albert to talk to his cousin, who just happens to be the king of Portugal!"

David laughed. Prince Albert was the husband of Queen Victoria. The Queen had clashed with Lord Palmerston in the past. How would their Royal Highnesses receive this proposal? How far above David's head all this maneuvering was now. It seemed to be at the very pinnacle of the British Empire! How could the Missionary Society ever hope to accomplish such a thing as this on its own? David had never been drunk in his life, but he now felt giddy with the power the British Empire possessed. But he knew in his heart this power—like drunkenness—could move from giddiness to disaster in an instant.

The Missionary Society did not send the letter to Moffat until April. This constant delay seemed to confirm David's decision to break away. He waited to do it though. Who could know if the government might run afoul of something?

In May, he was notified that the prime minister was considering a consulship for him, but it could not be effective until 1858.

If approved, his title would be "Her Majesty's Consul at Quilimane for the Eastern Coast and independent districts of the interior"—more or less. The salary of 500 pounds—five times his missionary salary—did not catapult him into wealth. His much younger brother Charles was receiving the equivalent of 750 pounds a year preaching in America. In fact, Charles was back in Scotland visiting. David urged him to stay awhile longer. He might be able to use him on his expedition.

The secret negotiations began to haunt David. The Society was proceeding on the notion he would be instrumental in establishing the mission with the Makalolos. Didn't David trust God? Why was he being so secretive? And with nothing final—neither his book nor his consulship—he suddenly resigned from the Society. He submerged in his writing, trying to remain oblivious of the public controversy over his resignation.

By the end of July, he finished the manuscript of the book and began a tour of public speaking. He felt very independent now. A woman's criticism of his concern with trade, as if that had nothing to do with Christ—drew this fiery response:

> Nowhere have I appeared as anything else but a servant of God, who has simply followed the leading of His hand. My views of what is missionary duty are not so contracted as those whose ideal is a dumpy sort of man with a Bible under his arm. I have labored in bricks and mortar, at the forge and carpenter's bench, as well as preaching. . . .

He spoke to scientific societies, physicians, and factory workers in towns and cities as far apart as London and Glasgow and Dublin. To his own cotton-spinners in Blantyre, many who remembered him from twenty years before, he said:

> My great object was to be like Him—to imitate Him as far as He could be imitated. We have not the power of working miracles, but we can do a little in the way of healing the sick, and I sought a medical education in order that I might be like Him. . . .

At Cambridge University at the end of his plodding factual speech, he suddenly shouted, "Do you carry on the work which I have begun? I leave it with you!"

Murchison told him later that the students and faculty at Cambridge were electrified by his speech. They were talking about establishing a joint missionary effort with Oxford University, just for Africa. *What a fine uplifting friend Murchison is,* thought David. He thought his own speech was a stumbling failure.

By November, he had finished "spouting off," as he called it, and his fat 687-page book, crammed with maps and drawings, was in print. It was titled *Missionary Travels and Researches in South Africa.* He had to laugh. He showed a copy of the tome to Mary. "Do you think anyone will read such a monstrosity? But at least a goodly portion of my sixteen years of work is preserved in print."

The book was not in print long. . . .

FIFTEEN

David was right; his book did not stay in print long—the first printing of twelve thousand books sold out in a few hours to advance orders. After that the English were buying the book as fast as it could be printed.

"God's work pays well," said Mary, as though it were preposterous.

"Suddenly our assets have grown from nothing but the clothes on our backs to several thousand pounds," agreed David. "Now I can support Mother. The children are assured now of decent educations. That is important to a Livingstone. And it's worth everything to me to know you will never suffer again from want, Mary."

Mary smiled. "And knowing you, a good bit will go to Africa."

"Perhaps we can help your father start his mission among the Zulus. And I hear your brother John may go to that mission. Naturally, I would have to help him, too."

"Naturally."

David soon learned that John Moffat was appointed to the Zulu mission. He wrote to him, offering him not only money, but his own wagon and ox-team. Characteristically, he urged John to proceed at once and not wait on a decision for every step of the process. Get on with it! A few days later he learned his advice had been too strong. John resigned from the Missionary Society, expecting to be funded by David. What choice did David have now but to do it?

From a London newspaper Mary, trying not to smile, read David a review of his book. "This reviewer says it is 'a narrative of great dangers and trials, encountered in a good cause, by as honest and courageous a man as ever lived.'"

"Who would write such puffery?" replied David uncomfortably.

"Charles Dickens."

The praise seemed never to end. He had already been received by the Prime Minister, who used the occasion to officially announce his consulship and expedition up the Zambesi River. Now in February of 1858 David was summoned to Buckingham Palace. In a large drawing room sat Queen Victoria, a tiny pinch-faced woman of forty, engulfed in a huge satin gown.

"Do sit down, Doctor Livingstone," she said. "Let me have a close look at the most famous man in the British Empire."

David was startled. He had grown numb from praise. He refused to listen to it any more. But what startled him was that Queen Victoria was probably right. He shook it off. "At last, Your Royal Highness, I can tell my African brothers I have met my chief. They never believe me when I tell them I have never seen my chief."

"Now that you have seen me, what do you suppose they will want to know about me?"

"Oh, that's easy, Your Royal Highness. They will want to

know just how many cows such a great chief owns."

Nothing could top his visit to the queen. David regretted every minute now he had to spend in England. His need for Africa burned in his heart like a fire. He had one last task; he appealed to his old friend from Glasgow, James Young, to administer the royalties from his book. Young, who now lived in London, agreed to see that his mother and the three older children had sufficient funds.

In March of 1858, David sailed on the *Pearl* for Cape Town with Mary and their only child not in school, Zouga. The elaborate plan to explore the Zambesi River was well under way. The British government had built a special low-draft paddle-wheeler for the Zambesi and loaded it in three sections aboard the *Pearl*. Also aboard were David's hand-picked men, not the least of which was his brother Charles as his assistant. Norman Bedingfeld had been selected as the ship's captain. The geologist Richard Thornton was recommended by Murchison, the botanist John Kirk by Sir William Hooker. An artist, an engineer, and a crew of ten were to be added later.

Robert Moffat met the *Pearl* in Cape Town in April. Mary would return with him to Kuruman. In 1860, Mary would go north to Kolobeng to visit the grave of daughter Elizabeth then continue north to join David on the upper Zambesi in the realm of Sekeletu and the Makalolos. The lower Zambesi was too unhealthy for Mary. David would not tolerate such a risk.

"Back at long last!" greeted Robert Moffat. And he hugged Mary, his daughter he had not seen in six years.

As David speculated earlier, after Robert Moffat received the much delayed letter from the Society in July, he had rushed to the Zulus to get their approval. He had only been back in Kuruman a few days when he left for Cape Town. Moffat was a phenomenon himself. Now sixty-three, he still traveled the wilderness fearlessly. He still was the only white man respected by the notorious Zulu chief Mosilakatse. Like David, he was so earnest and so honest he could win the confidence of anyone.

"I saw my son John on his way to Kuruman," remarked Robert Moffat. "It seems he has left the Mission Society, too," he added sourly.

"The fault is mine," admitted David. "I did not encourage that action, but something I said to John caused it to happen."

"How could John do that after being educated by the Society?" sighed Robert Moffat.

"There is always risk in Africa," answered David unsympathetically.

"Thank God John didn't take the mission among the Makalolos." Robert Moffat frowned, then smiled as he remembered. "Your Makalolos are still in Tete, David. Waiting for you."

"They have been waiting almost two years," said David with admiration.

"It seems we all wait for you," said Mary, with no humor in her voice.

Ten days later, the *Pearl* sailed around the tip of Africa for the Zambesi. Once again David was without Mary, but he could not take her into the fever country of the lower Zambesi. When he arrived at Quilimane, he learned he had been voted a Fellow in the Royal Society. The honors mounted. But he had no time to bathe in their warmth.

By June, the low-draft paddle-wheeler was assembled and named: *Ma-Robert*, the natives' name for Mary, the mother of Robert. Charles and the artist Baines got river fever almost immediately. Captain Bedingfeld turned out to be a complainer. And as they worked their way up the Zambesi, they found themselves in the middle of a war between the Portuguese authorities and rebel natives. David walked a tightrope trying to stay on good terms with both sides. On one occasion, David helped the sick Portuguese governor to safety as bullets whistled around him.

Captain Bedingfeld's hostility became so corrosive to the crew that David dismissed him. David could navigate the ship. And their Scottish engineer George Rae knew more than the captain about the workings of the vessel anyway. The *Ma-Robert* soon proved to be a poor ship at best. Only the hardest wood, acquired with backbreaking labor, fired the furnace hot enough to power the steam engine.

David was dismayed. "The ship holds only a two-day supply of fuel, and it takes four hours of that supply to build up enough steam to move just one inch!"

In September when they reached Tete, David's loyal Makalolos almost sank the *Ma-Robert* with their welcome. To his sorrow, thirty of them had died of smallpox and six had been murdered. Yet the rest, numbering over seventy, were not anxious to return to Linyanti. They held steady jobs in Tete and lived in stone barracks generously supplied by Major Nunes.

Relieved from any urgency to return the Makalolos to Sekeletu, David decided to push on to the Kebrabasa Rapids. Their presence had haunted him for two years. Impassable rapids were the one thing that could destroy his dreams of a watery highway into central Africa. So the paddle-wheeler *Ma-Robert* built up steam for four hours and wheezed up the Zambesi—at full speed not fast enough to keep pace with a canoe.

Within two days, David saw the Kebrabasa Gorge. "Doctor Kirk," he said to the most helpful man on his staff, "the Kebrabasa Rapids do not look promising."

John Kirk was speechless. It was a period of low water. There was such a jumble of granitic boulders a twig couldn't negotiate the rapids without striking a thousand of them. David anchored the ship and they proceeded up the gorge on foot. Each step added to David's misery.

Kirk finally found his voice. "During the rainy season in March, the roiling water would tumble a boat into kindling. In the dry season, the boulders would smash a boat into toothpicks."

David sighed. "I'll take four Makalolos and go on up the gorge. Perhaps the rapids don't stretch very far. One can ford the rapids for a short way, just as one can at Victoria Falls."

"Doctor, it's an insult to leave able-bodied men behind," protested Kirk.

"Able-bodied, are you? Well, come on then." David could hardly keep from smiling. Years ago he had walked Bakaa warriors into the ground. But how broken down by river fever was he at forty-five?

They proceeded into the jumble of boulders. Progress was exhausting. The gorge was very hot and the men had to jump from boulder to boulder. The boulders were so large there was no grip. And the surface was scorching. Soon even the four Makalolos were complaining. Kirk pointed out to David that their feet were blistered. David did not stop. Soon only Kirk and one Makalolo were still stumbling along behind him through the boulders. They climbed into masses of boulders that made even David wonder if he could ever get out. At one point they reached a cascade so bad the only way to continue on was to scale a 300-foot wall of slippery rock. They continued. The rapids went on and on.

Finally at one rest stop Kirk said, "The bottoms of my boots are worn out. They were brand new when we started."

David groaned. "I believe now these rapids continue for thirty miles!"

They started back, consoled only by the fact they were starting back. Fifty years before, the Portuguese could have warned David of the extent of these terrible rapids. But now they rarely ventured far from Tete. David returned to Tete. He would go downriver to Sena and follow the very large tributary Shire to the north. Perhaps the Shire River went north, then swung west to eventually bypass the rapids and join the Zambesi. David had seen stranger behavior in African rivers. He and Kirk would leave the others in the party at Tete. Most were sick with river fever. His prissy brother Charles was an embarrassment, requiring a dozen rest stops a day to do anything.

By January 1, 1859, when the *Ma-Robert* steamed up the duckweed-choked Shire against the advice of the Portuguese, David had regained his optimism. "You know, Kirk, I think we can make it up the Kebrabasa Rapids during high water. Of course, we will need a more powerful ship. I wrote Murchison about it."

Kirk's silence betrayed what he thought.

They took the *Ma-Robert* as far north on the Shire River as the village of Chief Chibisa of the Manganjis. They were above the low-lying fever country. This area David now optimistically dubbed the Highlands of the Shire. The residents, the Manganjis, spoke a different dialect of Bantu, which he immediately resolved to master. From Chibisa's village, he and Kirk trudged north on foot. They found an unwelcome but splendid cataract in the Shire, which David named Murchison Falls after his loyal friend.

Exploration of the Shire River would take almost all of 1859 and three separate trips north to satisfy David. As always, he seemed to know how to calm villagers, whether the villagers were threatening him with spears or not. By September he and Kirk had found two inland lakes hidden in precipitous mountains. The smaller one was Lake Shirwa, which appeared to be over fifty miles long.

At the south end of the larger Lake Nyassa, David asked a native, "How far north is the other end of this lake?"

The native was astounded. "Who ever heard of such a question? If a small boy started walking north he would be an old gray-haired man before he reached the other end."

"Balderdash," muttered Kirk. But when they climbed a considerable mountain to peer north, the lake stretched beyond the horizon.

Of the original crew only Kirk and the engineer Rae were productive. The geologist Thornton and the artist Baines were crippled by fever from the beginning. They could not function. David dismissed them. He had little sympathy for victims of river fever because he had suffered dozens of attacks himself. He believed a cheerful attitude and activity defeated illness, at least enough to continue working. As to medication during the awful bouts of fever, he wrote:

> [Mix]. . .resin of jalap and calomel of each eight grains, quinine and rhubarb of each four grains. . . [and take a] dose of ten to twenty grains. . . . If the violent symptoms are not relieved in four to six hours a desert spoonful of epsom salts may be taken. . . . Quinine in four to six grain doses. . .is generally given till. . . deafness is produced.

That was how drastic his treatment was. Deafness was welcomed by David as the last symptom before recovery. He was then on the go immediately. He drove himself that way constantly, and he had no sympathy for malingerers. Yet he could not bring himself to dismiss his lazy brother Charles. The morale of the other travelers was not helped by David's special treatment of his brother. The grumbling never stopped. How David wished he could work alone again, or perhaps with a common spirit like his sweet Mary, or John Kirk, who never seemed to tire, either.

David began to have problems with hemorrhoids. This kind of bleeding was not a problem one talked about. So he bore the pain and hid his problem from the others. He revealed his problem only to his diary. At times, he bled all night. The *Ma-Robert* was disintegrating, too. And he learned the London Missionary Society was sending missionaries to Sekeletu. It was too soon. He needed to be there to make sure Sekeletu moved into a higher healthier climate for Europeans, like the area around Zumbo.

But not all the news was bad. In November, he got a letter from Kuruman. "Mary gave birth to Anna Mary! Praise the Lord," he yelled. "It was one year ago: November 16," he added in surprise.

He redoubled his appeals for a new ship, now touting commerce on giant Lake Nyassa. He also had to get back to Sekeletu. The status of the new missionaries worried him. He soon learned his lectures at Cambridge and Oxford had caused such enthusiasm the two universities started a "Universities Mission to Central Africa." So they really were electrified; it was not just flattery. Missionaries were coming to the land around Lake Nyassa he called the Highlands of the Shire. David was really worried now. His appeals had triggered too much activity too soon. These new missions had to be tended with utmost care. How could he possibly attend to missions separated by a thousand miles of rough wilderness—and still explore for his river highway into central Africa?

Only twenty-five Makalolos wanted to return to Sekeletu in May of 1860. David didn't get back up the Zambesi to Sekeletu until August. He and Kirk were none too early. The young chief was a complete invalid with a severe form of eczema. Sekeletu was a sea of scabs. David and Kirk cleaned the sores with zinc sulfate, then daubed them with silver nitrate. Every day they gave him a powder of rhubarb, soda, and quinine to drink with water. He improved markedly but remained in the grips of the disease. The outlook was grim. When his white shaman left, Sekeletu would deteriorate.

Sekeletu's realm was in a shambles. He had refused to move out of the feverish swamps because the Zulus would not attack him there. The only reason he ever agreed to move to a higher healthier area was because he thought David would be with him. He reasoned shrewdly that if David lived with him the Zulus would not attack him because David was the son-in-law of Robert Moffat, the great friend of the Zulus.

Kirk found the missionaries at Linyanti. "Come with me, Doctor Livingstone. I've found the missionaries."

There was nothing there but a cemetery. Two families, including five children, had arrived among the Makalolos in 1859. By March of 1860, fever had annihilated all but one man and two children, who managed to straggle back to Kuruman. David was soon to learn the Makalolos, falling apart under Sekeletu, were indifferent to the plight of the missionaries. The natives refused to believe they were connected with David.

"Not that they could have cured the poor missionaries of fever anyway," concluded David objectively.

After only one month, David returned to Tete with a

heavy heart. Mary could not join him at Linyanti now. The land of the Makalolos was no longer a prospect for a mission at all. He must explore the Shire and make sure the new missionaries there would be safe. On the way back he impulsively tried to shoot the Kebrabasa Rapids in canoes. It was a disaster. No lives were lost, but Kirk lost eight volumes of botanical notes and everything he owned but the clothes on his back. How he regretted his words of many months before. He had learned only too well it was no insult to be left behind by Livingstone. It was mercy.

By July of the next year, 1861, the *Pioneer,* David's new ship, had arrived. And so had new missionaries for the Highlands of the Shire. They settled at Magomero with Chief Chigunda of the Manganjis. But the area was in great unrest. A tribe called the Ajawas were capturing natives and selling them as slaves. And soon after the missionaries arrived, they were faced with a heartbreaking decision. They heard Ajawas were in the immediate area leading dozens of captives in chains.

David was there with his Makalolos, too. "I've refrained from direct intervention in tribal squabbles whenever possible," he cautioned Bishop Charles Mackenzie, the thirty-six-year-old leader of the missionaries.

"But we can free these captives. I'm sure we are strong enough with your Makalolos. Just how badly do you want to stop slavery, Livingstone?"

David remembered how he had confronted Mpololo years ago. He couldn't argue that he never intervened in tribal conflicts. He found himself swept into an assault on the Ajawa slave party. In his heart, he had to think this day, too, he was compelled by God to free captives.

The rescue was easy. His Makalolos were as feared as the

Zulus. The Ajawas fled. The missionaries freed eighty-four captives. Bishop Mackenzie was elated. "We've shown the Ajawas that slavery will not be tolerated in this area."

David felt uneasy. Mackenzie's group was as bold as the group in Linyanti had been timid. Before he left to explore Lake Nyassa, he warned Bishop Mackenzie that taking sides in native wars was very dangerous. "I've reflected on our recent interference, and it must be the exception that proves the rule," he cautioned.

He explored north, compiling observations on every aspect of Africa. Once in the bush, he was charged by a rhino, which mysteriously stopped just before it reached him, as if it had encountered a stone wall. Then it sauntered away as if nothing had happened. To David, it was God's Unseen Hand again, and he noted the incident in his diary. Once he and Kirk would have been jumped by a crouching lion if one of the Makalolos had not warned them in time. David never recorded the incident in his diary. That sort of close call just happened too often.

Some observations were tantalizing. He noted that where river fever was prevalent, mosquitoes were abundant. But how would he ever find time to conduct an experiment? And when David found Lake Nyassa was not only thirty miles wide but went north for three hundred miles, he postulated a chain of lakes that went all the way to the Dead Sea!

On their way back from the upper reaches of Lake Nyassa, David was alarmed by the changes he had seen along the shores of the lake in just two years. The natives had thinned out. They were not disappearing from disease or famine. They were being shuttled away in chains. He was seeing the diabolical activity of the slave trade.

When he returned to Magomero in November, he had

news from the missionaries that shocked him. Mary was on her way to the Zambesi from Cape Town.

"No!" he blurted.

SIXTEEN

But it was true. Mary was coming to the mouth of the Zambesi with the wives of the missionaries. "Oh, Lord," he prayed, "protect Mary from river fever. When the ladies arrive, I must get them to the Highlands of the Shire as quickly as possible."

On January 31, 1862, David held his wife in his arms again. "Mary, at last!"

"It's been four long years," she gasped.

David was only too aware he had to get her out of this low-lying fever country. She could go with the other ladies to the mission at Magomero in the Highlands of the Shire. Later, she could stay there while he explored Lake Nyassa—or even go with him to the upper Zambesi realm of Sekeletu. Perhaps it wasn't too late to help the Makalolos after all. With Mary at his side he could do wonders. He liked to explore, but somehow the lower Zambesi had turned into a burden. Supervising other Englishmen was not his cup of tea—but more like a cup of bitter gall.

David LIVINGSTONE

"I must get you up to the Highlands with the other ladies," he said.

"After four years apart? Not on your life."

"But I have to stay here to get the new steamer ready." In the same ocean vessel with the ladies was the steamer David had ordered with his own money. He was going to call it *Lady Nyassa*. He had great plans for the lake.

"It won't take that long to assemble, will it?"

"In Africa? One never knows."

But Mary won the argument. The other ladies were quickly taken to Magomero in the Highlands. And the assembling of *Lady Nyassa* and unloading of their supplies from the ocean vessel dragged on and on. Unloading ships off the mouth of the Zambesi was very difficult and dangerous because of the shallow sand bars. David remembered only too well those very same sand bars had drowned seven men of the *Dart* in 1855.

Shocking news came from Magomero. The wives of the missionaries came upon a tragedy. Coming to meet them, Mackenzie and another missionary had been waylaid by a torrential rain. Both men had sickened and died from exposure and hunger. Was the young mission in danger of collapsing?

Mary shook her head. "My father once told you that no mission should be started unless one of the two of you could personally attend to it."

"At the time, I thought your father was immodest. But how right the wily old veteran has always proved to be."

By April, David and Mary were still in the lower reaches of the Zambesi. Mary could not be sent to Magomero. The mission there seemed to be disintegrating. The missionary Scudamore was down, crippled by river fever. Nothing was going right. And on April 21, Mary became sick at the village of Shupanga. Within hours she showed an extremely virulent form of river fever. Vomiting prevented the restorative powers of quinine. She faded so fast, David gave up on his medical care and prayed. Mary was a mere forty-one years old. But she was very worn down.

In six short days Mary Moffat Livingstone was dead. She was buried beneath a massive baobab tree in Shupanga on the Zambesi River. David wrote in his journal:

> *It is the first heavy stroke I have suffered, and quite takes away my strength. I wept over her who well deserved many tears. I loved her when I married her, and the longer I lived with her I loved her the more. God pity the poor children. . . . For the first time in my life I feel willing to die. . . . I have often wished that [my resting place] might be in some far-off still deep forest, where I might sleep sweetly till the resurrection morn. . . .*

The next two years were profoundly depressing. The Portuguese were now openly hostile to David as they realized how ardently he opposed slavery. They also suspected correctly he had suggested to the British government a British colony around Lake Nyassa. To make matters worse, David learned that Sekeletu had died and the disheartened Makalolos were scattered by the Balondas. To make the times overwhelmingly tragic, the natives from the Zambesi River to Lake Nyassa were being annihilated by slavery, war, and famine. Bodies bobbed in the Shire River as human flotsam. The Universities' Mission at Magomero was hanging on by a thread.

On March 19, 1863, David's fiftieth birthday, he and Kirk were rushing up the Shire River to the mission. Scudamore had died. Dickinson was gravely ill, and Clark was hysterical. Only

Horace Waller was healthy. David and Kirk arrived too late to help Dickinson. Clark was doctored back to sanity, but the mission now seemed doomed. David's work on the Zambesi was not faring much better. Kirk and David's brother Charles were giving up on the work. What a drastic change in fortune for David from ten years earlier. And how his own health had suffered, almost from that fortieth birthday. David had endured ten years of river fever and now had a new thorn in his side: bleeding. Yet he could write to one of his fellow missionaries:

> *Thanks for your kind sympathy [about the death of Mary]. In return I say, cherish exalted thoughts of the great [missionary] work you have undertaken. It is a work which, if faithful, you will look back on with satisfaction while the eternal ages roll on their everlasting course. The devil will do all he can to hinder you by efforts from without and from within; but remember Him who is with you, and will be with you always.*

Yet, occasionally, he began to suspect that not only was his support from England and South Africa vanishing, but his time on earth was running out, too. In one letter he wrote *I don't know whether I am going on the shelf or not. If so, I make the shelf Africa. . . .*

David's only tangible accomplishment in the two years after Mary's death was exploring the Rovuma River six hundred miles up the coast from Quilimane. He suspected it might be an easier access to Lake Nyassa. And he could skirt the Portuguese. He was wrong. The river was far too shallow.

"I must go back to England," he told himself. "I'll stay with the children for a while."

But what would he do with *Lady Nyassa*? He couldn't bear

to scuttle it. But if he left it, slave traders would surely get their hands on it. In typical fashion David solved the problem with a radical solution. He would sail the *Lady Nyassa* 2,500 miles across the Indian Ocean to India! The engineer Rae, a good hand for so many years and the only man with real experience at sea, refused to go on such a suicide mission. "Doctor Livingstone! If you don't get there in time, the monsoons will blow you right to the bottom of the ocean."

Yet off sailed David with a totally inexperienced crew of three white men and nine African natives in the *Lady Nyassa*. During the voyage he recorded his gloomy thoughts:

> *Often wish that I may be permitted to do something for the benighted of Africa. I shall have nothing to do at home; by the failure of the Universities' mission my work seems in vain. . . . Have I not labored in vain? Am I to be cut off before I can do anything to effect permanent improvement in Africa?. . . God grant that I may be more faithful than I have been, and may He open the way for me.*

Just as the monsoons struck forty-five days later, David anchored the *Lady Nyassa* in India. He found people in Bombay to care for the Africans, left his steamer in the care of a British Naval officer, and embarked on a ship for England. He arrived in London July 23, 1864. He was publicly criticized for his roles in the failure of the Universities' mission at Magomero and in the tragedy of the London Missionary Society's mission at Linyanti. But his main supporters, Roderick Murchison and Prime Minister Palmerston, staunchly defended him. After all, they had financed his Zambesi exploration, which was the prime reason he was not free to shepherd the new missions.

He went on to Scotland to see his children, his sisters, and his mother. His arrival was no more timely than it had been with his father years before. His mother was senile, thinking he was a grandson. The visit was not all gloom. He saw his daughter Anna Mary for the first time. She was almost six years old. She took more to her uncle Charles, who was back, too, because he was more affable than David. *If only people knew,* thought David, *how miserably Charles acted in trying circumstances.* Charles had actually kicked Makalolos in his temper tantrums.

In Glasgow, David consulted the best physicians in Scotland about his recurrent bleeding. He did not like their diagnosis. His hemorrhoids were so severe he needed an operation. It was not a difficult operation, but recovery was very slow. Time was so precious. David refused to have the operation. He was a doctor himself.

"I'll keep the bleeding under control," he assured himself.

In Bath, he spoke to the British Association about the evil role Portugal played in slavery. Thousands of natives were dying in wars triggered by slave traders. Thousands of natives were disappearing in the ships of the slave traders. England should establish a colony around Lake Nyassa and stop the evil practice. His public denunciation of Portugal was very dangerous. He had to go back to that region of Africa where the Portuguese ruled.

He returned with daughter Agnes to London to write a second book. David was especially fond of Agnes, who was seventeen and no longer in school. They were guests in Newstead Abbey, the home of William Webb, whom he had met in South Africa. David worried about his oldest son Robert, who had tried to join David in Africa. After Robert could not find him, he had impulsively sailed to America, only to find himself fighting for the Union in their Civil War.

In the meantime Murchison urged him, "Return to Africa as a geographer only. You spread yourself too thin. Projects are failing because you try to do too much."

David refused. "I evangelize while I explore. I would give up exploring before I would give up evangelizing."

The new year of 1865 was sad. The Livingstones learned that Robert had died of battle wounds in America. If only Robert could have found David in Africa. But at least Robert died in a cause that David loved himself: ending slavery. Later that year, David's mother died. To add to his misery, the sales of his second book, *Narrative of an Expedition to the Zambesi and its Tributaries,* were puny compared to the first book—not that he cared much for money, but money fueled his exploration. And there wouldn't be any more books. He didn't think he would ever come back to England.

But old friends rallied around him. Murchison raised funds for his next expedition from the Royal Geographic Society. The British government matched that amount. And James Young matched the total of those two donations. David jokingly called his old friend Sir 'Paraffin' Young because he had patented a method to extract paraffin from coal. Clean-burning paraffin was now the major constituent of all candles. James Young was very wealthy.

In September 1865, David returned to India to sell *Lady Nyassa* and recruit porters for Africa. Then he sailed to the mouth of the Rovuma River and pushed west. Even if the river was not navigable, he had to establish a new route to Lake Nyassa around the hostile Portuguese on the Zambesi. He had sixty porters, a mix of Indians and Africans of various tribes. After Lake Nyassa they pushed on to the west. How he loved finding a new village in the high country, waiting, parleying,

preaching the gospel, then pushing on to the next village.
He enthused in his diary:

> *The mere animal pleasure of travelling in a wild unex-*
> *plored country is very great. . .brisk exercise imparts elas-*
> *ticity to the muscles, fresh and healthy blood circulates*
> *through the brain, the mind works well, the eye is clear,*
> *the step is firm, and a day's exertion always makes the*
> *evening's repose thoroughly enjoyable. . . . The effect of*
> *travel on a man whose heart is in the right place is that*
> *the mind is made more self-reliant: It becomes more con-*
> *fident of its own resources—there is a greater presence of*
> *mind. The body is soon well-knit; the muscles of the*
> *limbs grow as hard as a board and seem to have no fat;*
> *the countenance is bronzed and there is no indigestion. . .*
> *the sweat of one's brow is no longer a curse when one*
> *works for God [but]. . .actually a blessing. . . .*

But this trip was very different from any other. The
porters were insolent, with no common bond. Some of them
were inexplicably cruel to their animals, actually beating donkeys and oxen to death. They began to desert David. Within
six months only eleven men remained. And David found he
had passed from one slave trading realm into another. No
longer were the Portuguese the instigators. These new slave
traders were Arabs.

In spite of his problems, he was over a hundred miles
west of Lake Nyassa by the end of 1866. Losing most of his
porters was an improvement. His remaining eleven men were
tried and true. Two of the most loyal were Susi, a native from
Shupanga, and Chuma, a young Ajawa who had gone all the
way to India and back with David.

The next years were spent roaming hundreds of miles west of Lake Nyassa. It was not aimless. David discovered two more lakes: Moero and Bangwelo. He took his careful geographic measurements, described animals, recorded each village and its events, preached the gospel, then pushed on. He had some interest in finding the source of the Nile, since it was now widely known it had to be somewhere deep in central Africa. What a stroke of good fortune it would be if he could establish trade in central Africa by a Nile River route. Who would have believed it?

In 1869, after recovering from his first bout with pneumonia, he trekked to Ujiji on Lake Tanganyika north of Lake Nyassa to find mail and send mail. Then he pushed on to the west. His lungs were weak now. Fever struck off and on. Bleeding dogged him. He lost his front teeth, loosened by eating rock-hard corn on the cob. His men dwindled to six. Yet he could write in early 1870:

Caught in a drenching rain which made me. . .sit,
exhausted as I was, under an umbrella for an hour try-
ing to keep. . .dry. As I sat in the rain a little tree-frog,
about half an inch long, leaped on to a grassy leaf, and
began a tune as loud as that of many birds, and very
sweet. . .so much music out of so small a musician. . . .

Soon he heard he was very close to a mighty river thousands of feet wide and very deep, flowing north. The Manyuema natives called it the Lualaba. He could not know for sure if it flowed north into the Nile or the Congo. The Congo was an anathema—worse than the Zambesi. The Congo River was already known to become unnavigable only eighty miles from the Atlantic Ocean. Raging cataracts stretched upstream as far as English explorers had cared to follow them—for at least one hundred miles. But David would follow this Lualaba downstream by canoe.

"Soon I will know for sure if it flows into the Nile or the Congo," he said with great anticipation.

Then he was crippled by ulcers on his feet, which refused to heal. Only Susi, Chuma, and another man remained. Although David could almost smell the great Lualaba, he had no choice but to recuperate. At the village of Bambarre, during months of forced rest, he read the Bible four times. But he read Psalm 46 so often the ink was disappearing:

> God is our refuge and strength, a very present help in
>   trouble.
> Therefore will not we fear, though the earth be
>   removed, and though the mountains be carried
>   into the midst of the sea;
> Though the waters thereof roar and be troubled, though
>   the mountains shake with the swelling thereof.
>   Selah.
> There is a river, the streams whereof shall make glad
>   the city of God, the holy place of the tabernacles of
>   the most High.
> God is in the midst of her; she shall not be moved: God
>   shall help her, and that right early.
> The heathen raged, the kingdoms were moved: he
>   uttered his voice, the earth melted.
> The LORD of hosts is with us; the God of Jacob is our
>   refuge. Selah.
> Come, behold the works of the LORD, what desolations
>   he hath made in the earth.
> He maketh wars to cease unto the end of the earth; he

breaketh the bow, and cutteth the spear in sunder;
he burneth the chariot in the fire.
Be still, and know that I am God: I will be exalted
among the heathen, I will be exalted in the earth.
The LORD of hosts is with us; the God of Jacob is our
refuge. Selah.

Other favorite Psalms were numbers 23, 40 through 43, 90, 95 through 113, and 121. He could not bring himself to read the book of Job. He felt as if he were living the life of Job. He was white-bearded now, more and more toothless, weak-lunged, lame, and very emaciated. He had long ago forgotten about his maimed left arm. His objectives had never changed. He would expose the slave trade in every way he could, and he would tell Africans about Jesus. And there was the never-ending hope that he would find some great navigable river in the interior that flowed all the way to the ocean. If honest trade could reach the natives, it would mean the end of slavery and the beginning of Christianity.

In January of 1871, Chuma heard a rumor in the market-place. "There is a party of white men searching for Doctor Livingstone."

David laughed. "The marketplace is full of rumors. I'm in better health now. We must move on to the great river we've heard about. If it's not a rumor, too."

Then they found it. The Lualaba was truly thousands of feet wide. Soon David was resting in Nyangwe, a very large Manyuema village on the river, negotiating for canoes to take them downstream to explore the river. Nyangwe was the most corrupt village he had ever seen, frequented by Arab slave traders and cannibals. One man wore a necklace of ten human jawbones. He brandished a knife and boasted how he sliced up his victims and ate them. When David blistered him with condemnation, the man laughed and laughed.

But David relished most natives and their marketplaces. This one had about three thousand buyers and sellers in it most days. While staying at any village he made it a point to stroll through the market often, reassuring the natives of his kindness and good intentions. At Nyangwe, he wrote in his dwindling supply of paper:

> . . .my going among them has taken away the fear engendered by the. . .slavers. . . . Each is intently eager to barter. . .the sweat stands in beads on their faces. . .cocks crow briskly and pigs squeal. . .the men flaunt about in gaily-colored lambdas of many folded kilts—the women work the hardest—the potters slap and ring their earthenware all around to show that there is not a single flaw. . . . It is the scene of the finest acting imaginable. . . . Little girls run about selling cups of water to the half-exhausted wordy combatants. . . . I see new faces every market day. Two nice girls [today] were trying to sell their. . .roasted white ants [termites], called gumba. . . .

One sultry afternoon three months later, David was in the market listening to innocent haggling over fish, palm-oil, chickens, pigs, salt, pepper, and clay pots. But real anger erupted as three Arab slave traders squabbled with a Manyuema woman over a chicken.

Suddenly, gunfire popped!

SEVENTEEN

Bullets whistled past David.

"Duck!" he yelled as he tumbled to the ground.

The three Arabs were firing into the throng. Then guns were heard exploding from every direction. All the other slave traders must have joined the fray.

When the fusillade ended, David rose to see several hundred Manyuema were dead and dying, mostly women. He heard many had tried to escape into the Lualaba and drowned.

David hobbled to the Arab leader Dugumbe. "It was all planned ahead of time by you Arabs," he screamed. "All this blood is on your hands. You wanted to terrorize them and your devils jumped at the first excuse. How long do you expect to get away with these outrages against God?"

"Stay out of it, Doctor," said Dugumbe coolly. He prided himself on being very civilized. "You are a very good man. May God go with you."

The stench of evil in the area nauseated David now. The canoes were controlled by Arabs, too. How could he ever explore the river now? His supplies were low and he remembered the search party Chuma had heard about in January. So he and his faithful three natives trudged back to Ujiji on Lake Tanganyika.

By October of 1871, David was camped in Ujiji. Ujiji was also under the fist of the Arabs, but their atrocities here were more subtle. David was reduced to making notes on the backs of scraps of newspaper. He made crude red ink out of the seeds of a plant. To the people in the village this strange old white man's prospects were dismal. But David trusted God with all his heart and soul.

Then one morning Susi came running. "An Englishman! I see him!"

"An Englishman?" replied David. "Is it possible?"

He rose to stare ahead. A caravan of porters heaped with supplies came toiling into the dirt streets of Ujiji. Flying above was the American flag. A young man of about thirty-five strutted ahead of the caravan. Guided by Chuma he headed toward David's hut.

The young man stopped in front of David and asked, "Doctor Livingstone, I presume?"

"Yes." David tipped the gold-banded blue cap he always wore.

"Thank God I have been permitted to see you, Doctor."

David smiled. "Thank God I am here to welcome you." There was a sad note in his voice. "Come under the verandah. Have a seat." David waved at a straw mat covered with goatskin.

The young man sat. "I'm Henry Stanley, Doctor. I've talked with your old friend John Kirk, the British Consul of Zanzibar."

"Kirk! How is he?"

"Fine. I have something for you. Mail." And Henry

Stanley had one of his men bring a bag of mail to David. David placed it on his knee and waited politely. "Please, Doctor, read your mail," insisted Stanley.

"I've waited years for mail. I can wait awhile longer."

But Stanley persisted until David read mail from his children. Agnes was going to be married. Tom was very sick. Then Stanley told him the news of the day: The Suez Canal opened; the Americans had tied their distant coasts with a railroad. As he talked, David's suspicions of the young man dwindled. Stanley knew all about David. He knew all about David's friends and had talked to them. Stanley had managed a very rough journey from the port of Bagamoyo near Zanzibar. David could see he handled himself very well with natives. David learned Stanley had been with the British Army when it moved against the king of Ethiopia. Stanley had fought in the American Civil War. David warmed to him. Perhaps Robert would have been like this young man, had he not been killed in the same war fighting slavery.

David read the rest of his mail that night. Robert Moffat and his wife were back in England. At seventy-six, Robert was still active. David's strongest convert Sechele still ruled the Bakwains. In London, Lord Clarendon had died. William Thomson, the young son of the mathematics professor at the University of Glasgow when David was there so many years ago, was knighted. He was now Lord Kelvin, one of the most famous physicists in the world.

"Quite a little group in that chemistry laboratory back in Glasgow so many years ago: Sir Paraffin Young, little Willie Thomson, now Lord Kelvin and, of course myself, the old wheezer of Africa." He chuckled. Mail was such a wonderful tonic.

His old friend Murchison still supported him, garnering

yet more funds for supplies. The Royal Geographic Society had even transported parts of a new river boat for him to Lake Nyassa and assembled it there on the lake. But when would David ever get back to Lake Nyassa?

The next morning the young man said, "I represent the *New York Herald.*"

"So that's what you do. What is a newspaper correspondent doing here?"

"I was sent here to look for you."

"Do Americans care that much about me? How very odd. Well, I'm thankful you came. My supplies are gone. I am almost reduced to begging."

David began to feel so much better that he and Stanley explored the northernmost end of Lake Tanganyika together. Stanley bought him a donkey to ride because of David's horribly ulcerated feet. But help from the donkey was limited. Hemorrhoids prevented David from riding most of the time. On one excursion away from camp as he walked beside his donkey, they were attacked by fierce African bees. The poor beast dropped down and rolled in panic. David plunged into thick brush. Bees were in his hair and his clothes. Finally, the bees he hadn't crushed left him. He emerged from the brush. The donkey was stung to death.

Stanley's donkey had bolted ahead. Stanley had suffered only a few stings on his face. He was horrified when he saw David. "It's many miles back to camp, Doctor. Let me ride ahead and send the litter back for you."

"Too much of a bother," said David. "I can walk to camp by the time you send the litter back." His face and arms weltered with stings, he walked eighteen miles to camp.

That evening as David sipped tea, Stanley said, "Now I know why you've outlasted everybody in Africa."

"Oh, poppycock."

"I have seen only one face as grave as yours, Doctor," said Stanley. "It was Abraham Lincoln's."

"Poor Lincoln," muttered David ambiguously.

David did not like criticism or compliments. But he liked Stanley. Stanley was a trooper like Kirk. Only one aspect of Stanley's visit irritated him: Stanley's repeated appeals for him to leave Africa. In most disputes David politely refused and went about doing what he wanted to do anyway—with no explanation whatever.

But this time he confided in the younger man, "I feel sometimes as if I am only the first evangelist to attack central Africa, 'crying in the wilderness,' and that other evangelists will shortly follow. And after those, there will come a thousand evangelists. My way is very dark and dreary, but the promise in Psalm 37 is:

Commit thy way unto the LORD; trust also in him;
and he shall bring it to pass. And he shall bring forth
thy righteousness as the light, and thy judgment as the
noonday.

"I may fall by the wayside, being unworthy to see the dawn. I thought I had seen it when the Universities' mission started above the Zambesi, but the darkness settled again. The dawn will come, though. It must come. I do not despair of that day one bit. The whole earth will be covered with the knowledge of the Lord. And as far as the slave trade, my business is to publicize what I see and to rouse up those who have the power to stop it. The evangelists of the gospel will follow."

"But why not return to England, Doctor, and fully recover? Then you can come back and finish your work."

"Oh, I only look worn out. Many years ago I almost died in Luanda. Years ago I almost died in Tete. I've been sick every other day since about 1853."

"But that's eighteen years of hard use."

"I'm so close to my goal. I must go back and follow the Lualaba. Don't you see, Stanley? If I can only get the English traders into the interior, slavery will stop and Christ will triumph. I can't bear to think of all the souls being lost every day. I am so close. Why sail to England? I'm healthy again, thanks to you. Who knows but God? I could go down in a ship returning to England."

In March of 1872 Stanley left, carrying an enormous amount of correspondence from David, including his journals. He was also carrying David's full account of the massacre at Nyangwe. To David that was vitally important to get out. Surely the civilized world could not ignore such atrocities. David knew he could never find a more able or more trustworthy person than Stanley to get his mail to the outside world—which David had not seen for six years!

He waited stoically in Ujiji for supplies he knew would be sent now that Kirk knew where he was. In his condition, he no longer felt days of rest in camp were wasted. Only a certain number of days in the field were left to David. Only God knew how many.

He relaxed in his faith while he waited, writing his thoughts on its meaning:

What is the atonement of Christ? It is Himself; it is the inherent and everlasting mercy of God made apparent to human eyes and ears. The everlasting love was disclosed by our Lord's life and death. It showed that God forgives, because He loves to forgive. He

works by smiles if possible. If not, by frowns; pain is
only a means of enforcing love.

He was ecstatic when a letter arrived to tell him that
Henry Stanley arrived safely in Zanzibar. Another letter griped
that Stanley was going to gain his fame and fortune off David's
reputation. David remembered how Stanley had shared everything he had with David—right down the middle. He wrote a
fellow missionary:

> *[Stanley] behaved as a son to a father—truly overflow-*
> *ing in kindness. The good Lord remember and be gra-*
> *cious unto him in life and in death. . . . [As to the sug-*
> *gestion Stanley will make a fortune out of me] he is*
> *heartily welcome, for it is a great deal more than I*
> *could ever make out of myself.*

David was saddened by a letter which told him Roderick
Murchison had died. In his heart, he considered Murchison
his staunchest friend. Proof of that soon arrived in the form
of supplies. In August 1872, David left to go south to the end
of Lake Tanganyika then strike west to the upper reaches of
the Lualaba considerably upstream of the Arab slave traders.
Never before did David tire so easily. Never before did he
have dysentery so often. Never had he been so constantly
wracked by pain. It was in his very bowels now. And most
grave of all, never had he bled so often. Yet he continued his
long standing ritual: approach a village, send word, wait, par-
ley, tell of Christ, move on. . .

Around the south end of the lake, he and his loyal three
headed west into a marshy nightmare. For several months,
they slogged through muck. It rained daily and progress was

very slow. Once, with grim humor, he noted in his diary:

> *A lion. . .wandered into this world of water and ant-*
> *hills, and roared night and morning as if very much*
> *disgusted; we could sympathize with him!*

March 19, 1873, was his sixtieth birthday. Ten years before he had been rundown and depressed on his fiftieth. But that fiftieth birthday seemed festive compared to this birthday. His poor health began to frighten him. He knew he should have plenty of years left. His father had enjoyed sixty-eight years, his mother and both grandfathers well over eighty years. And the last time he had letters from the outside world, his older brother John was still alive and in good health. But the bleeding worried David. Still, as long as he rested occasionally for a few days and rebuilt his strength, he should be all right. After all, he was a doctor. So on his sixtieth birthday he wrote hopefully:

> *19 March—Thanks to the Almighty Preserver of men*
> *for sparing me thus far on the journey of life. Can*
> *I hope for ultimate success? So many obstacles have*
> *arisen. Let not Satan prevail over me, Oh my good*
> *Lord Jesus!*

By April 1873, however, entries in his diary were unrelentingly grim:

> *10 April—I am pale, bloodless, and weak from bleed-*
> *ing profusely ever since the 31st of March last; an*
> *artery gives off a copious stream, and takes away*
> *my strength. . . ."*

Entries in his diary became ever briefer:

*21 April—tried to ride, but was forced to lie down and
they carried me back to the village exhausted.*
22 April—carried in kitanda *[stretcher]. . .S.W.
[southwest] 2 1/2 [hours of travel].*
23 April—ditto. 1 1/2 [hours].
24 April—ditto. 1.
25 April—ditto. 1.
*26 April—ditto. 2 1/2. To Kalunganjofu's, total [for
week]. . .= 8 1/2 [hours of travel]*

On April 27, near the south shore of Lake Bangwelo and
the village of Chief Chitambo, he was too sick to travel at all.
His hut was hastily built in drizzling rain. Boxes of supplies
supported his sleeping mat above the muck and slime.
Chitambo came the morning of April 30 to pay his respects.
David was too weak to talk to him but implored him to come
back the next day. Surely with rest and goat's milk, he would
recover his strength. He had been flat on his back before—a
hundred times.

Later he heard much shouting and called Susi, "Are our
men making that noise?"

"No, Doctor, the villagers are driving a buffalo out of their
fields."

Pain was agonizing now. He had Susi bring his medical
box. With Susi's help, he took a dose of calomel. Perhaps that
would help. When he was alone again, he crawled off his bed,
and on his knees leaned forward, resting his elbows on the
mat. He was bleeding profusely.

He prayed, "Let God's will be done."

The pain subsided. Yes, surely it was God's mercy for the

doomed, just as he had felt the pain subside so many years ago in the jaws of the lion. Now he was in the grip of Paradise. Glory must be minutes away.

He ended his prayer, *"For to me, to live is Christ and to die is gain."*

The great moment approached. He had not failed. He felt the presence of his dear wife, Mary. Glory, at last. . .

AFTERWORD

Susi and Chuma buried David Livingstone's heart and internal organs under a *mvula* tree. They preserved his body with salt and sun-dried it for two weeks. They wrapped it in calico, then tree bark, then sail cloth. They lashed that bundle to a pole and tarred it air tight. They and other natives then carried the bundle for eight months—all the way to Zanzibar—over one thousand miles.

On the way, a stranger encouraged them to abandon the bundle. Chuma explained, "No. This is very very big man!"

The HMS *Vulture* was sent to carry his body to England. On April 18, 1874, Livingstone was buried in Westminster Abbey among the other legends of Britain. Over a period of thirty-two years in Africa he had walked, crawled, climbed, waded, canoed, boated, ridden, and been carried over 40,000 miles of the "white man's grave." He took notes and made maps every step of the way. He told every African he saw the good news about Jesus Christ.

His father-in-law Robert Moffat said, "He sacrificed

everything—home, Christian intercourse, lucrative prospects, and earthly honors—for one grand object, to carry the gospel of the Son of God to the heart of Africa."

Livingstone had such power from the Holy Spirit that in the remotest areas Africans, who cared nothing for anyone's honors in the white world, spoke of him decades later.

In 1990, the ten modern African countries where Livingstone trod the old native trails had a population of over 140 million. Of the 125 million nonwhites in that number, a staggering total of 75 million are Christians. *There are today millions upon millions of nonwhite Christians in the part of Africa that got its first taste of the gospel from David Livingstone. . . .*

FOR FURTHER READING

I. Two biographies stand out as comprehensive:
   Blaikie, W. G. *The Personal Life of David Livingstone.*
   London: Murray, 1880. There are many later editions,
   including one in 1986 by Barbour & Company.
   Seaver, George. *David Livingstone: His Life and Letters.*
   New York: Harper & Brothers, 1957. The best recent
   combination of biography and objective criticism.

II. Livingstone's own voluminous writings, in two forms:
   A. For popular reading:
   Livingstone, David. *Missionary Travels and Researches in
   South Africa.* London: Murray, 1857.
   Livingstone, David. *Narrative of an Expedition to the
   Zambesi and Its Tributaries.* London: Murray, 1865.
   Waller, Horace, ed. *Last Journals of David
   Livingstone in Central Africa.* London: Murray, 1874.

   B. Compilations from diaries and journals
   Schapera, I., ed. *David Livingstone: Family Letters,
   Vol. 1, 1841–1848.* London: Chatto & Windus,
   1959.
   ———, ed. *David Livingstone: Family Letters,
   Vol. 2, 1849–1856.* London: Chatto & Windus,
   1959.
   ———, ed. *Livingstone's Private Journals 1851–1853.*
   London: Chatto & Windus, 1960.
   ———, ed. *Livingstone's Missionary Correspondence
   1841–1856.* London: Chatto & Windus, 1961.